SCHOOL READY

SCHOOL READY

A practical and supportive guide for parents with sensitive kids

SONJA WALKER

'Sonja has written an incredibly practical book about a concern most parents wrestle with: ensuring their child is ready for school. This is an issue that confronts most parents before their child starts school, but is most certainly amplified for families with children with unique needs. Sonja combines simple, realistic advice that parents crave and her work is underpinned by her comprehensive experience as a former teacher and as a mum. Sonja has a thorough understanding of the latest research and science about child development and balances this with personal stories and anecdotes interspersed throughout the book. This is a must-read for all parents and early childhood educators embarking on the journey of preparing children for school.'

Dr Kristy Goodwin, Digital Health and Wellbeing Speaker, Researcher, author and mum

'As a mother of three, all with unique needs of their own, and a primary teacher of 30 years, I can relate to this sensitive and realistic book. Sonja has thoroughly covered the many aspects and concerns about your child starting school from a parents' point of view. She has given suggestions of how to deal with so many situations in a humorous, sensible and practical way. Personal and professional anecdotes throughout the book add a personal and very real touch to what can be a traumatic and deeply stressful time of life for all parents, and especially for those with sensitive and unique needs. A thoroughly enjoyable, informative and practical read. I wholeheartedly recommend this book to any parent of a child that is starting school.'

Tracey Nicholls, Primary Teacher

'Sonja Walker is a dynamo and this book not only reflects her years of service to kids and families, but also her personal integrity and passion for representing families whose voices are rarely heard. Readers of *School Ready* will benefit from the commonsense wisdom of this hard-working professional who is an amazing source of knowledge for Australian parents.'

Mary Klarica, Speech Pathologist

'As a teacher, I wish every parent could read Sonja Walker's book *School Ready* before their child starts school. *School Ready* is an invaluable resource for families and preschool and school staff because it is clear, concise and comprehensive. It addresses some of the issues that aren't often spoken about at orientation days, and provides parents and carers with the encouragement they need to be a strong and sensible advocate for their child not only in their first year of school, but for their entire educational journey. Sonja Walker just "gets" kids and families. Her wealth of experience in education, coupled with her ability to share her knowledge in a warm and compassionate way, is second to none.'

Vickie Dean, Primary Teacher

'As a teacher and a mum of four kids I know first-hand how passionate Sonja is about giving every child the opportunity to be the best they can be. Her book offers practical advice that is easy to read and gives parents the encouragement they need to be successful advocates for their children as they navigate their way through the school years.'

Lisa Neate, Learning Support Teacher

'Here is a book that deals with the realities of choosing a school. It demystifies the sometimes "secret school business processes" that cloud our decision making and shows parents how we can best navigate the sometimes daunting road of education for our children.

'Sonja provides clear facts for many situations we may find ourselves in as parents, but more importantly, speaks from personal experience, which has given her real insight into the struggles of parents of students with varying needs, and the challenge faced during the crucial periods of a child's early school life.

'Sonja nails every point with clarity and a genuine love of what is best for any student/child, but especially for the sensitive or diverse student/child.

'An accessible book for any parent but also any school that wants to ensure they provide the best for their yearly intake of new students. Her explanations of various areas we as parents and teachers are often concerned about are clear, concise and easily understood. The strategies are effective, and manageable.'

Henrietta Stathopoulos, Education Officer – Drama, Sydney Catholic Schools Performing Arts

'This book is a practical, "no holds barred" guide. It will help you not only help get your child ready for school, but help you to be ready also. You can use the book to reflect on areas that you may not have thought about while walking you through the things that are bothering you. Sonja's use of stories from families as well as teachers shares personal insights that are personal and immensely valuable. I think that families, intervention services and schools alike should look at ways to use it.'

Kerry Dominish, Early Childhood Interventionist, Speech Pathologist

'For years, I've been looking for a high-quality school readiness resource to share with parents of sensitive children, and from now on, this excellent book will be the one that I recommend to all of the families I work with. *School Ready* is an invaluable tool to guide parents through the important and stressful time of school selection and transition. Sonja Walker's helpful advice echoes the sentiment of clinical supports I provide in psychology consultations with families, so I am thrilled that this invaluable resource will be available to all Australian families. The wisdom and guidance Sonja shares in *School Ready* is essential reading for parents and professionals alike.'

Caroline de Fina, child psychologist, Founder, Best Start Clinic

First published in 2018 by Sonja Walker

© Sonja Walker 2018
The moral rights of the author have been asserted

All rights reserved. Except as permitted under the *Australian Copyright Act 1968* (for example, a fair dealing for the purposes of study, research, criticism or review), no part of this book may be reproduced, stored in a retrieval system, communicated or transmitted in any form or by any means without prior written permission.

All inquiries should be made to the author.

A catalogue entry for this book is available from the National Library of Australia.

ISBN: 978-1-925648-63-8

Project management and text design by Michael Hanrahan Publishing
Cover design by Peter Reardon

Disclaimer
The material in this publication is of the nature of general comment only, and does not represent professional advice. It is not intended to provide specific guidance for particular circumstances and it should not be relied on as the basis for any decision to take action or not take action on any matter which it covers. Readers should obtain professional advice where appropriate, before making any such decision. To the maximum extent permitted by law, the author and publisher disclaim all responsibility and liability to any person, arising directly or indirectly from any person taking or not taking action based on the information in this publication.

CONTENTS

Foreword xv

Introduction 1
    I've been there too   1
    A view from both sides of the desk   3
    Kids First   4
    Sensitive children with unique needs   4

PART I: REALITY CHECK

1   How to choose the right school   9
    The different schooling options   10
    Beware of bright shiny objects   11
    What does your child need?   11

2   Does the school book match its cover?   21
    What to look for when you visit a school   21
    Your child may change schools later   24

3   Knowing what to expect   27
    What are your expectations?   28
    Your child will follow your lead   29
    Good communication is vital   30

4 The big switch: preschool vs primary school 33
Dealing with larger class sizes 33
Building responsibility and independence 34
Working with more than one teacher 35
Getting ready for the playground 37
Learning that losing is okay 40

5 10 top tips to help your child succeed at school 45
Top tip 1: Teach your child to ask for help 47
Top tip 2: Talk about feelings 47
Top tip 3: Play Sweet 'n' Sour 49
Top tip 4: Have your child's speech and language checked six months before school starts 51
Top tip 5: Create a school story for your child 53
Top tip 6: Use your child's favourite characters 56
Top tip 7: Visit the school informally 57
Top tip 8: Attend orientation days 58
Top tip 9: Get insights from your child's early educators 59
Top tip 10: Tell the school what it needs to know 61

6 At what age should my child start school? 65
Starting ages across the country 66
There is much more to school readiness than chronological age 67

PART II: DEVELOPING GREAT RELATIONSHIPS WITH TEACHERS AND OTHER PARENTS

7 Creating understanding at school 77
Understanding is a two-way street 78
Now *that's* a knife 79
Share the good stuff too 82
Things will be different 83
School is new for you too 84

Contents

8 Six ways to get connected at your child's new school 85
How to develop strong relationships within the school community 86
Other things you can do 90
There's no hurry 93

PART III: FITTING IN AND MAKING FRIENDS

9 Finding belonging and acceptance 97
What were your school years like? 98
Finding belonging 99
Finding acceptance 102
Protecting your privacy 106
Have realistic expectations 107

10 Finding friendship 109
The ability to make friends is a learned skill 110
Friendship skills start at home 113
Preschool is a good start, but … 114
'Who did you play with today?' 115
Tips for positive playdates 116
What's Harry Potter got to do with it? 117

PART IV: CLOSING THE GAP

11 Don't leave me! 121
Separation anxiety is more common than you think 122
Mums and dads hold the key 123
Separation anxiety is difficult to overcome 125
'See you later' strategies 126
Six top tips to learn to say goodbye 126

12 Number ones and number twos   131
    Skipping to the loo isn't always easy   132
    School readiness tips that you've probably never heard before   134

13 How to help a fussy eater   143
    Food fights   144
    Sending out an SOS   145
    How to feed your fussy eater at school   146
    Ask teachers to be your ally   150
    Try not to talk about it   151
    Get help if you need it   152

14 How to manage meltdowns   155
    Your child's brain is still on its 'L' plates   157
    Kids are like a cup   159
    Manic mornings   160
    Strategies to manage meltdowns   161
    Putting a drain in your child's cup   162
    Find out what works for your child   166
    Other people will only understand when you do   167

PART V: MAKING YOURSELF HEARD

15 How to speak up without shouting   171
    Knowing where to begin with teachers   172
    When to start the conversation   172
    What to take with you   173

16 The best times to talk to teachers   175
    Parent–teacher nights   176
    Picking your moment   177
    Letting teachers know what you want to talk about   178
    First and last week fails   180
    Avoiding report time   180

Contents

17 Who's who at school?   183
     The principal's role   184
     Who else can you call?   185
     It takes two to have a conversation   190

18 Top tips for parent–teacher interviews   191
     Top tip 1: Send an email first   192
     Top tip 2: The KISS principle   193
     Top tip 3: The power of a 'cc'   193
     Top tip 4: Never meet alone   194
     Top tip 5: Help me to understand   196

Conclusion: Lifeboats and safety nets   199
     The ship's captain   200
     Elastic band kids   201

Local education authorities   203

Helpful resources   213

FOREWORD

It is both an honour and a privilege to be asked to write a foreword for this book.

I first met Sonja a few years ago when trying to find therapists who could help my children, who both have unique needs and needed more support within the school environment and at home. In that time, I have grown to respect Sonja for the incredible wealth of knowledge she has, as well as her passion and drive for helping not just the hundreds (if not thousands) of children who come through her doors every year, but their parents as well.

Being a parent of a child with unique needs can, at times, be both confronting and difficult. On the other hand, there are many moments of jubilation and reward as you see your child reach a milestone other parents might take for granted, or where something you have been patiently trying to teach your child, they suddenly learn to do! At other times, it can be frustrating or heartbreaking – particularly when you see your child struggling and you don't know what to do; those moments that leave you feeling helpless to support your child.

I have seen Sonja help parents in situations when they have felt lost and unsure of what to do next. I have also been a recipient of Sonja's care and compassion in those moments, and have been so grateful for her support and wisdom. *School Ready* is a collection of that wisdom, and the many years of experience that Sonja holds within her. I couldn't be happier that she has made the decision to commit all of this incredible wealth of expertise to paper in a book that can now be shared far and wide with so many other parents. Whether you are looking for advice, or direction, or you are just trying to prepare yourself and your child for school, you will find what you are looking for within the pages of this book.

Kylie Ouvrier
Parent

INTRODUCTION

On 31 January 2006, my red-haired, blue-eyed baby boy started school. He was almost five, and his backpack was nearly as big as he was. I was a first-time school mum, but I was also a qualified teacher, and so when he was born I thought that helping him grow up and go to school would be a breeze.

What I didn't know was life had other plans for him, and for me too.

I'VE BEEN THERE TOO

My little guy's developmental differences were identified when he was three and a half, but I'd known that something wasn't quite right well before that. He'd been slow to speak, very fussy with food, and on the go from the moment he could walk. In those early years I did everything I could to encourage him to 'use his words', from taking him to parks so he could improve his social skills to organising playdates with friends so that he could connect with other kids. But despite everything I did, I still endured countless conversations with exasperated early educators who seemed to take every opportunity they could to pull me aside and talk about the problems he was having, and causing, in the playground.

It was a brutal start to motherhood, and I spent many sleepless nights agonising over what I was doing wrong.

The fact that my son was an only child probably didn't help. Ironically, I had taught plenty of sensitive students with unique needs in my classroom years. I was the teacher who put her hand up to teach the children who struggled. Children who had learning difficulties and kids whose social and emotional skills were a bit immature were just my cup of classroom tea. Over the years, I taught boys and girls whose personalities were a bit left of centre, kids who came from complicated families, twins and even triplets. My classrooms were filled with students who had anxiety, ADHD, and kids whose first language wasn't English, and I loved them all.

But the reality was that I had never started from scratch with a child of my own, and I have to admit becoming a mum was a bit of a wake-up call. I thought I knew what I was doing, but as my son started experiencing difficulties at preschool it became apparent to me that I didn't.

So I did what many mums do – I blamed myself.

It was easy to load myself up with the responsibility for his challenges. I worked full time and was the primary wage earner for our family. My son was lovingly cared for by his doting grandparents and fantastic dad, but I could only take him to playgroup once a week and so my 'working mother guilt' was on overdrive.

None of my close friends had small children, and I didn't have anyone to compare my son with. I secretly wished I could be like the

Introduction

other mums I knew, the ones who worked part time or had been able to stay at home instead of returning to work. No matter how many books I read or parenting courses I did, I just couldn't quell the secret worries I had for him.

Getting ready to start school was meant to be easy, but for my child it wasn't working out that way, so that had to be my fault, right?

So you see, I've been where you are. As a mother, I've felt the very real worry, fear and frustration that comes from feeling that teachers, other parents and even school principals just didn't 'get it'. I've looked for information that I couldn't find, and asked for advice from people who weren't able to give it. I know exactly what it's like to feel desperately worried about a child whose needs are just a little bit different, and I have first-hand experience of the challenges of starting school with a sensitive child who has unique needs.

A VIEW FROM BOTH SIDES OF THE DESK

I've also been in places that you perhaps have not been, and so that's why I'm glad you're reading this book.

As a teacher, I've sat on the other side of the desk at parent–teacher interviews. I've taught kids of many ages and abilities, and on occasion I've had to have difficult conversations with mums and dads. I've worked in staffrooms where the needs of children are discussed and planned for by their educators. As a classroom teacher, I've experienced the challenge of trying to meet children's individual needs while simultaneously dealing with constraints such as insufficient time, funding and resources. Many of my dearest friends still work in Australian schools, and I know the landscape that today's teachers navigate is immensely challenging.

There's no doubt that knowing how 'the system' works in schools has helped me support my child, and I hope the practical ideas and

insights I will share with you here will give you the head start you need as you embark on your child's journey to school.

KIDS FIRST

Equally, I hope you will receive value from the advice and resources I will share as a result of the work I do now. For more than a decade, I have had the privilege of leading an experienced team of children's health and education professionals in a practice I established in 2007 called Kids First Children's Services.

At Kids First, my colleagues and I specialise in helping children and families get ready to meet the challenges life throws at them. Every day I work with psychologists, speech pathologists, occupational therapists and teachers, and together we give parents and kids the commonsense strategies, guidance and support they need to thrive and not just cope.

SENSITIVE CHILDREN WITH UNIQUE NEEDS

For some children, making a successful start to school is about much more than lunchboxes, uniform labels and early literacy skills. For your child, a successful start to school might mean finding ways to manage their anxiety, cope with their sensory sensitivities or manage the social and emotional demands of the playground. Or it might mean finding ways to cater for cognitive differences, such as learning difficulties or giftedness.

Your child might be one of the many who is starting school next year who has physical, health or dietary needs that require extra understanding. Or your child might come from a family background that is a little complex.

Introduction

Perhaps your son or daughter has experienced situations that other five year olds have not, or your family is new to Australia and you are unfamiliar with what starting school entails.

We often hear the cliché 'all children are unique', and of course that's true. But when it comes to starting school, it's not always easy to find school readiness solutions for the unique problems that set children like yours and mine apart from their peers.

So as you read this book, take heart.

For every problem, there is a solution, but admittedly some are harder to find than others.

In the pages that follow, you'll read about real families who have kindly allowed me to share their 'going to school' experiences and insights with you. To protect their privacy, I've changed their names for this book. Perhaps their stories will resonate with you.

You see, there are many thousands of parents who have trodden the path that you are about to embark on with your child.

You are not alone.

I hope that this 'sensitive' guide to school readiness – full of ideas and tips from experienced teachers, health professionals and parents – will help you and your child make a happy and successful start to school next year.

Sonja Walker
May 2018

PART I

REALITY CHECK

The first year of school is called different things in different places in Australia, so if you were educated overseas, that fact alone might already have you confused.

Where I live in New South Wales, children start Kindergarten, or as it's affectionately known, 'Kindy', on their first day. If you live in Victoria, Queensland or Tasmania, your child might be heading off to Preparatory, or 'Prep', next year. South Australian children go to Reception. Western Australian kids go to Pre-primary, and Northern Territory school starters go to Transition. Confusing, huh? If it's okay with you, I'll refer to 'Kindergarten' or 'Kindy' in this book and hope that you'll know what I mean.

The title given to the first year of formal schooling that your child will enter next year is possibly just one of many things you are trying to get your head around right now. If you haven't set foot in a primary school playground in decades and your child is starting school next year, you'll probably notice that things have changed quite a bit since you were a student yourself, and you may notice that the way schools are run differs too.

Today's classrooms contain technology that hadn't even been invented when we were kids. The curriculum has evolved to include subjects you've possibly never heard of too. The structured play that characterised the Kindergarten classes of years past are long gone, and these days kids start learning from day one.

Knowing this can make getting ready to start school just that little bit more complex for the sensitive children of parents like you and me. For us, the process doesn't just start with buying a backpack and pencil case in December and skipping off to the local school in January.

For us, the thinking, planning and (let's be honest) worrying started months – or even years – ago.

Heading off into the uncharted territory of school can be daunting, and if concerns about what school will really be like for both your little one and for you are playing on your mind now, those little niggles are only going to get bigger unless some of the mystery about 'Big School' is removed.

So before we dive into the nitty gritty of making sure your sensitive child with unique needs makes a successful start to school, let's take a quick reality check so that the questions you're asking get the answers you need.

CHAPTER 1

HOW TO CHOOSE THE RIGHT SCHOOL

'Before I had James, I worked in a busy corporate role where I managed big projects, and when I look back, I see that choosing a school for James became another project for me. I started collecting school prospectuses when he was six months old and I spent years agonising over the options available to us. I made complicated spreadsheets so that I could compare one school with another and I developed my own quality assurance checklist to fill in when I did school tours. I even gave principals a score out of ten based on my impression of their leadership skills. My husband told me I was overthinking things, but I couldn't help it. I felt that our decision about James's school was going to be a big factor in his future and I just didn't want to stuff it up.'

Karen, James's mum

James was born when Karen was 43. As an older mum, she felt that he would probably be her only child and she freely admits that – from the moment she knew she was pregnant – she put all of her energy into making the most of her one and only chance at motherhood.

I wish I had a dollar for every parent who has asked me about how to choose the right school for their child. I'd be a wealthy woman who spends her days luxuriating in a beachside paradise where the words 'Mum, where's the … ?' are never heard.

But seriously, if you're feeling anxious about what school to send your child to, you are not alone.

It's such a big question because there is so much riding on it, and it's very common for parents to be seeking answers for it well before the year their child is scheduled to start school. After all, the school you send your child to now could be the one that siblings attend in the future, and as a family it's possible you will be part of the community there for a decade or even longer, so it's absolutely natural to want to get it right the first time.

THE DIFFERENT SCHOOLING OPTIONS

As the parent of a sensitive child with unique needs, it's quite easy to become bamboozled by information and possibilities. Depending on where you live, the options might be many or few. Regardless, doing your homework early will give you the best chance of making an informed choice for your child.

If you live in a metropolitan area, you might have the luxury of options such as schools run by your state's Department of Education, faith-based schools such as your local Catholic, Anglican or Islamic school, or independent schools that cater for children from specific language or cultural backgrounds. You might be in-area for schools that base their teaching and learning on educational philosophies such as the Steiner or Montessori models. If your child has a disability, you might be looking at schools that offer special education support, and if your child is gifted, you could be considering schools that select students on the basis of academic merit.

BEWARE OF BRIGHT SHINY OBJECTS

These days, many schools offer tours for prospective parents. They might be led by the principal, assistant principal, or even the marketing manager if the school is an independent one with a healthy promotions budget.

It can be easy to be impressed by the things I call 'bright shiny objects'. Swimming pools, sports grounds, music rooms, theatres and computer labs offer wonderful facilities for kids, but as parents of a child with unique needs, I encourage you to look beyond them. There is much more to a school than its buildings.

It's also natural for schools to put their best foot forward when they are showing you around. You're likely to tour the facilities which staff are most proud of and visit classrooms where its most dynamic educators and settled students are teaching and learning. The students you meet will probably be boys and girls who are hand picked for the task of impressing guests with their vivacity and eloquence too.

WHAT DOES YOUR CHILD NEED?

The important question to ask yourself before you start looking at school websites, talking to neighbours or visiting schools to determine their relative merits is, 'What does my child need?'

Think about your family's values and priorities. Does the school you are considering place importance on the qualities you subscribe to? Do you feel that, as a family, you will feel welcome in the school community? Do you get the sense that, if you or your child needed support, you would feel heard? What can you do to make sure you 'scratch under the surface' and find out what you need to know? My advice is to ask specific questions, and lots of them, because specific questions get specific answers, and you'll need this information to make considered choices for your unique child. Every parent wants their child to have the very best chance of being happy and successful at school, and you and I are no different. Choosing the right school is important for every child, but when your child has unique needs, that choice does take on extra significance.

I know you're probably keen to start visiting schools. You've got your clipboard ready and you may even think that Karen's quality assurance checklist is a jolly good idea. But there are a few things that would be useful to do first. Touring schools without an idea of what you're looking for is like going to the Boxing Day sales without a shopping list. You're likely to be impressed by almost everything you see and come home more overwhelmed than when you started.

Questions to ask yourself

Before you start asking questions of principals and teachers, it's a good idea to first think about, talk through and clarify your answers to some fundamental questions about your child that only you can answer.

- *What are your child's strengths?*

    Every child has things that they are good at and interested in. Your child probably has character traits that make them unique and special too, such as a curious mind, a sensitive and creative spirit, or even the ability to speak more than one language. Knowing what your child's strengths are is the first step towards finding a school that will nurture your child's talents and passions.

- *Which of your child's skills need extra encouragement or support?*

  As a parent who is thinking so very carefully about your unique child's transition to school, you are the expert in their needs. Teachers who have never met your son or daughter will seek your insights, and the more you share, the better they will be able to help. What specific struggles does your child have? What triggers those moments of challenge? How do you manage it at home? What advice have you received from professionals who have supported your family? Having a strong idea about these things will make it easier for you to have effective and productive conversations with the teachers you meet during school visits.

- *What kind of temperament does your child have?*

  Is your child a gregarious extrovert or a sensitive, creative soul? Does your child enjoy a boisterous, busy environment or does noise and activity cause your child to withdraw? Does your child take change in their stride or need predictable routines in order to manage their behaviour? When we talk about your child's temperament, we are talking about how your son or daughter reacts to the world around them. As parents, we usually have our child's personality and temperament well worked out by the time they start pre-school, so this is worth keeping in mind as you plan visits to prospective primary schools.

- *Is going to a school that is part of your local community important to you?*

  What are you, as a family, hoping for as your child starts school? Is being able to walk or ride their bike to school

important? Would having local friends be easier for social and practical reasons, such as birthday parties, playdates and emergency pick-ups if you get stuck at work? How would your child cope with a commute to school if they had to travel more than 30 minutes each way by public transport? Is the structure, philosophy and opportunity offered by an out-of-area school more important to you than the convenience of a school that is close to home? Would it be easier for you if your child went to school close to where you work, or where other members of the family live? Your child is going to be at primary school for six or seven years, so it really is worth thinking about the long-term consequences of the decision you make about the location of your child's school. If possible, you are probably going to want your child to stay at one school for the duration of their primary education, so I encourage you to look at all of your options and to have a 'long range' approach to your planning.

- *What social, cultural or religious values are important to your family?*

  The point that I always come back to when talking with families about choosing a school is their family values. There's nothing worse than sending your child to a school that espouses ideas or beliefs that you don't subscribe to. It could be confusing for your child to be taught concepts at school that you don't believe in at home, and it could make interaction with the school uncomfortable if you are not prepared to attend and support events that are considered highly relevant there. So, does the school that you are considering for your child have a philosophy that is consistent with yours? If you have worked this out before you visit, you are likely to get a 'gut' feeling about it almost immediately, and you will know if it's the right community for you and your unique child to join.

Questions to ask school staff

Once you have a clear idea about your child's needs and the type of environment that will best meet them, it's time to start visiting schools.

Remember, specific questions are more likely to receive specific answers, so here are a few you might like to ask as you meet with teachers, principals and parents as you search for the school in which your child will thrive.

- *How many students are enrolled in the school?*

    The size of the school could be significant for your sensitive child with unique needs. If the school has a very large population, what will that mean for playground interactions or the management of your child's anxiety or sensory issues? If the school is a very small one that caters for only one class group in each year, will it provide your child with sufficient social, creative, sporting and learning opportunities? The answers you receive to these questions could end up being important factors in your decision making.

- *How many teachers does the school have?*

    If learning is difficult for your child, this could be another make-or-break question. Schools with a big team of teachers often have more capacity to offer extracurricular activities that offer 'non-academic' kids the chance to shine. A small school with a tiny staff team simply might not have enough hands on deck to offer the same breadth of outside-the-classroom opportunities, so the answer you receive to this question might have significance for your child. When querying the composition of the school's staff, it's also worth asking if students have access to support staff such as a school counsellor or psychologist. These specialist staff are often

shared among schools, and so the school you are considering may have this person on site every day, or they may only have their services once or twice a week. In the years to come, this extra layer of support within the school could be valuable for your child and family.

- *How many classes have teachers who job share?*

    Teachers who job share work part time, and this means their students are usually taught by two educators. You may wish to think carefully about whether this structure would suit your sensitive child. Often children in their first year of school are offered the stability of one teacher, however schools sometimes allocate teacher teams to classes in Years One to Six. If you think your child might struggle in a class where teachers job share, make sure you ask about the composition of other grades within the school.

- *Will any member of the School Executive be teaching Kindergarten next year?*

    School leaders often have responsibilities that take them out of the classroom, leaving their students in the care of substitute teachers. While members of the School Executive are often very experienced educators with a lot to offer to your child, you may wish to consider whether having an assistant or deputy principal as the teacher during your child's first year at school is in your child's best interests.

- *Does the school have a Learning Support Team?*

    Learning Support Teachers have specific qualifications and experience in assisting children who have different learning needs. If you feel that your child will need extra help, find out as much as you can about who is on the team and how your child might get access to their support.

- *How does the Learning Support Team support students, teachers and parents?*

    While every teacher needs to 'diversify' the curriculum to meet the needs of their students, they will often consult with the Learning Support Teacher or team to do this. Will you have a part to play? Does the school offer formal Individual Education Plans (IEPs) for students, and how often can you reasonably expect to be in contact with a member of the Learning Support Team to discuss your child's needs, learning and progress? So that you can have realistic expectations, the answers to these questions could be helpful as you make choices for your child.

- *Does the school use specific learning or wellbeing programs to support students?*

    Some schools implement school-wide programs designed to support behaviour and learning. Two popular examples are the Positive Behaviour Engaging Learners (PBEL) program in New South Wales and Victoria's School-wide Positive Behaviour Support (SWPBS). Other schools use a whole-school approach to literacy and numeracy or implement withdrawal classes using evidence-based literacy programs such as Multi-Lit. Does the school you are considering have programs of this nature? What would that mean for your child?

- *If you wanted your child to participate in support programs, what criteria would apply?*

    In any school there are often many children who are struggling, however resources are usually tight and teachers need to make tough decisions about which children receive support. Choices about how and when it is delivered need to be made too. It's worth asking about how children who receive support are selected and how long support can realistically be provided for.

- *What funding is available to support your child with unique needs?*

  This an important question to ask, and also to research on your own. Many parents expect that funding for a teacher's aide, playground support person, specific resources and teacher training is included when they sign their sensitive child up to school, but sadly that is rarely the case. If you believe your child might need extra help, this is not a question to ask in front of a crowd as you do a group tour of the school. It's not appropriate during a casual five-minute meet and greet with the principal either. If you are seriously considering enrolling your child with unique needs in the school, make an appointment so you can ask this confidential question. Do your research before your visit by learning about the funding options that are available in the state and education system you are considering joining, so that when you go to the school and ask questions about funding support, the answers you receive make sense to you.

- *What is the school's policy about in-school visits from therapists or other professionals?*

  Some schools welcome speech pathologists, occupational therapists, and hearing and vision support workers, and others do not. While it can be convenient to have therapy take place during school hours, remember the venues in which these sessions take place might not always be optimal for your child's learning. Lots of therapists I know report that they've conducted therapy sessions in all kinds of inappropriate spots, such as the photocopying room, a sports shed and even on the steps outside the library. If the school welcomes therapists, or even has them on staff, ask to see the room in which sessions take place so you can decide if that environment would meet your child's needs. Remember too that if therapy takes place at school you may not necessarily be there. You will need to decide if the convenience of in-school therapy outweighs the benefit of your involvement and direct interaction with your child's therapist.

- *What is the school's policy about being out of school to attend medical or therapy appointments?*

  Some schools have no problem with children arriving late or leaving early to attend medical or therapy appointments, but it's always worth asking the question. Schools do have compulsory attendance protocols which need to be respected, and so you may need to seek approval if your child is going to miss a great deal of school to attend regular appointments.

- *What extracurricular activities are available?*

  The great thing about starting school is that it opens a whole new world of possibilities for your child to find interests, abilities, talents and passions that give them confidence and a way of being acknowledged and valued within their community. Make sure you ask about the extracurricular activities or lunchtime clubs that are offered at the school. These can be a way of giving your child the chance to shine, and could also be the place where they find likeminded kids who will become their friends.

As you visit schools, remember that this is your best chance to get the information you need to make a conscious, informed choice for your child's primary school education. Don't be shy – teachers and principals are asked questions all day, every day, and they're used to talking about their school. Ask the same questions at every school you visit so that you can compare apples with apples, and don't forget, it won't just be *what* teachers say but *how they say it* that will be important as you meet them for the first time.

Your first impressions of schools will come not just from what you see, but also what you hear. As your questions are answered, you'll get a sense of how the school works and how the staff interact with parents. This in itself could be a good indicator as to whether the school will be a place in which your child and family will thrive.

CHAPTER 2

DOES THE SCHOOL BOOK MATCH ITS COVER?

Schools are quite good at presenting themselves in a positive light. They're familiar with having visitors in the school for open days and Education Week, and attracting students is particularly important for private and independent schools whose enrolments are not guaranteed in the way enrolments for government-run schools are.

Visiting a school is an important part of deciding whether to send your child there. So what should you look for during these visits?

WHAT TO LOOK FOR WHEN YOU VISIT A SCHOOL

As you visit the schools that you are considering for your sensitive child, keep your eyes and ears open for the subtle, but important, messages you will receive about the people your child will be in contact with next year. If you keep the following questions in mind during your school tour, you'll get an idea of the school's culture and whether it's a good fit for your child and family.

- *How do students and teachers interact?*

    As you move around the school, do you hear voices raised in anger or frustration? When you look into classrooms, are children busily (not necessarily quietly) engaged in learning activities? Can you spot any children who are cooling their heels outside the room because they've been sent out? How do the teachers and auxiliary staff speak to the children during incidental contacts such as in the playground or on the way to the library? Do the school leaders appear to know the children's names? All of these observations will give you an idea of the culture of the school and how well your child and family might fit in.

- *How welcoming are members of the front office staff?*

    I often say that the people who work in the school's front office secretly run the school. While school offices are not necessarily the exclusive domain of women these days, it's certainly true that they usually remain the heart and soul of the community. Often staff who work in the front office have been a part of the school for a very long time, know everything there is to know about it, and are the 'gatekeepers' to the teachers you want to talk to. Equally, when your child has forgotten their lunchbox, is feeling unwell or is struggling in the playground, the front office is likely to be their first port of call. Based on your observations during your visit, could your child go to these people if they needed assistance?

- *What opportunities are there for you to see the school at work and at play?*

    Open days, Education Week and school tours offer a great overview of schools, but often you can gain insight into the kind of community it is by visiting on other occasions. Does the school have a fete, fair, art show or creative arts performance that you could attend? Would you be welcome at a weekly assembly to see how the students behave and are spoken to by teachers? Ask the question and see what answer you receive. It will give you a good idea of the school's ethos.

- *Who conducts the school tour?*

    It's not always practical or reasonable for the principal to be available for spontaneously organised school tours, but if you meet the marketing manager, senior students or another member of staff, are they willing and able to answer all of your questions? If you meet the principal or another member of the school's leadership team, what impression do you get? How do other members of staff and students respond to them as you move around the school? The observations you make about the people you meet could be important in your decision making.

- *What was that person like?*

    Did the school representative you met seem to be the kind of person who you could turn to if you had concerns or if your child experienced difficulty? This is an important consideration for every parent, but for those of us who have children with unique needs, it's really worth thinking about. In any given school, there are people who hold different roles. If you or your sensitive child have problems that need to be solved, there are likely to be a number of staff you will turn to, and it's quite possible that the first person you will call is not the principal. I know this might sound odd, but these days principals are very often tasked with running the 'business' of the school. While they are dealing with budgets, HR and the implementation of policies and procedures, other members of the team – such as assistant principals, school counsellors and leading teachers – are the first options when worries arise. So my message here is not to be too concerned if you find that you meet a principal who seems a little preoccupied

or with whom you don't immediately 'gel'. Of course, if they come across as an authoritarian that staff and students are fearful of then take note, but there may be others in the school community that you are likely to have more to do with. Try to meet them too if you can.

If you were buying a house or a car, you'd probably take the time to research your options and make sure you were as informed as you could be before you signed on the dotted line. Choosing a school for your child has similar significance, because in handing your precious son or daughter over to teachers you are transferring your trust (and that is a hard thing to do!). Making the best possible use of school visits will help you to make confident choices, so be prepared to ask questions, and, if possible, take someone who knows your child with you when you do a school tour. Another person may notice things about the school and its staff that you don't, and it's good to be able to talk decisions through with someone who has their own perspective on what you have seen and heard.

YOUR CHILD MAY CHANGE SCHOOLS LATER

Sometimes we think that the first school we choose for our child needs to be their one and only forever school. But it doesn't always work out that way. Schools change, the people who lead them change, our children's needs change, and sometimes it becomes necessary to move to another school that will offer something new or better.

No parent ever wants to disrupt their child's schooling, but sometimes it happens, and as mums and dads we need to be okay with that. You might move away and it may no longer be geographically possible for your child to finish primary school in the place they started. Or you might need to move your child because they will be better off somewhere else.

Does the school book match its cover?

This has happened to my family twice. The primary school we loved lost the inspirational principal we'd met when my son started there, and by the time Year Five rolled around, bullies and an ineffective teacher made his life a misery. He needed a safer school, and so we had to find a new one for him. It wasn't easy, but it had to be done.

The same thing happened two years later in Year Seven, when the inflexible headmaster of the school my son attended demonstrated no understanding of his needs. The man mercilessly bullied my son and me, as well as the teachers who could have supported us. Getting out of that environment was the best thing we ever did for our child, and he is a happy, well-adjusted teenager today despite the trauma of that time in his life.

I have seen this kind of thing happen many times in my professional life. Children change schools for lots of reasons, but if they have your support, they often cope better than you might expect.

So, from personal and professional experience, may I encourage you not to get too caught up in your search for the perfect school? It doesn't exist.

What you can do, though, is look for the school that ticks most of your boxes now. The school that matches your family values and the one that will work with you to support your sensitive child with is the one you need to be working with and towards.

The future is a long way away and it will look after itself.

CHAPTER 3

KNOWING WHAT TO EXPECT

'I really didn't know what to expect when Braydon started school. I just hoped that they would see him for who he was and care enough about him to help him.'

Kerrie, Braydon's mum

Kerrie has two sons with unique needs. Diagnosed with autism when they were seven and four, her children Braydon and Noah are smart, funny and interesting boys who love buses, planes and being members of a model train club.

Like lots of mums and dads, Kerrie and her husband Pat have ridden the getting-ready-for-school rollercoaster. While Kerrie didn't know that Braydon had autism until he was in Year One, she was aware that his needs differed from his peers. In the months before school began, Kerrie hoped that Braydon's new teachers would have solutions to the problems he seemed to have.

A school and teachers that care is what every parent hopes they'll find for their child. If you are like Kerrie and don't know quite what to expect when your child starts school, you are not alone.

WHAT ARE YOUR EXPECTATIONS?

So, you've been visiting lots of schools, asking lots of questions, and perhaps even making lists of their comparative advantages and disadvantages. Now that you've narrowed the contenders down, working out what you are actually expecting from the school that you're sending your child to is an important step.

Are the hopes you have realistic, or are you setting a standard that the school and its teachers will never be able to achieve?

As a mum, I must admit I didn't really know where the boundaries were when my son started school. Having come from a supportive early intervention environment where I was guided and advised every step of the way, it was quite a shock to go into the school system where I was basically on my own. In the months before school started, I didn't know who was who at the school, what steps teachers would take before we arrived in January, and what I needed to action myself beforehand.

Although I was a teacher, it had been a while since I worked in a Department of Education school and I felt a bit lost and out of the loop. For some reason, I expected that the school would have automatic systems which clicked into gear when my child with unique needs enrolled in Kindergarten. How wrong I was.

Great expectations: know what the school can and can't provide

Like I did, you might have ideas about your child's new school that you haven't actually road-tested yet. You may be assuming that, because you have had a conversation with the school about your child's disability diagnosis, the principal will go ahead and apply for funding so a teacher's aide can be employed to assist your child. You might be expecting that, because your child's enrolment form has been submitted, extra staff allocations will be automatically available to support your anxious, ADHD or sensory-sensitive child at drop-off time or in the playground. You may think it's a no-brainer for an acceleration program to be provided for your gifted child, or an individual literacy support program to start immediately when your child with a language delay arrives.

Unfortunately, it doesn't work that way.

The fact is that schools, principals and teachers can't make these kinds of things magically appear like a genie from a bottle. There is a 'big picture' that we parents aren't always privy to, and schools have to take the needs of every child, teacher and class into account as they make plans for each intake of school starters.

When parents hold unrealistic expectations for what their child's school is able to implement, it's a recipe for disillusionment, disappointment and dissatisfaction. The last thing you need when your child starts school is to have difficult conversations with teachers about what you think should be happening. It's much better to discuss these things before school begins so that you know what teachers will be responsible for and what you need to implement and organise at your end.

YOUR CHILD WILL FOLLOW YOUR LEAD

A highly experienced teacher I know, who I will call 'Ashley' to protect her confidentiality, holds a leadership position in a K–12 school in Sydney. She says that the expectations parents bring with them can be decisive factors in the long-term relationships they and their child build with teachers.

'What some parents don't realise,' she says, 'is that schools are a system. They're a machine with lots of moving parts, and so they need to be administered from a big-picture point of view. Families, on the other hand, are small and operate as independent units, so the perspective that parents have is usually very specific. Schools and families sometimes have to meet in the middle, and this is something that parents who are new to the education system may not know when their child starts school for the first time.'

Ashley says that if misunderstandings between parents and teachers occur, children very quickly pick up on their parents' attitude towards the school.

'You wouldn't think it's possible for five and six year olds to be so perceptive, but often they are. The way parents speak about teachers and school when they are at home can affect the way their children respond in the classroom and playground.'

Sometimes, the easiest thing to do when there is a problem is to blame something or someone else for it, but if children do this they miss out on developing the skills they need to be responsible for their own learning. If your child is aware that you lack confidence in a teacher or the school as a whole, it can be easy for them to develop a bit of a 'victim mentality' which will get in the way of their resilience.

If you have concerns about any aspect of your child's schooling next year, be careful about what your child hears. Parents who project their doubts and opinions onto their children can affect the way their children perceive their teacher and school, and you wouldn't want that to happen, would you?

GOOD COMMUNICATION IS VITAL

As I prepared to write this book I spoke with a lot of teachers, and every single one of them told me that good communication and a willingness to compromise are the keys to managing everyone's expectations when your sensitive child starts school.

Remember, you and your family are joining a system. As much as possible, the staff who administer the school will do their best to support and accommodate you and your child's unique needs, but that willingness to listen and understand needs to work both ways.

Most of the teachers you will meet during your child's journey will be people whose hearts are in the right place. They do care, and that's why they chose a career in education in the first place. Occasionally, your child's teachers will be subject to processes and procedures that you may not be aware of or agree with, and they may not be able to give you the answers you want to hear.

As adults, it's important to try to understand the perspective of others. It's the only way we can enjoy collaborative relationships within the community that we and our child will be part of now and in the future. The outcomes your child achieves at school will not only depend on what happens in the classroom and playground, but also on the conversations you have at home and in the offices of the principal, deputy and learning support teacher.

We all hope for the best when we hand our children over to teachers, but it's important to have realistic expectations about what is possible and what is not. Your child will share the teacher's attention with a big group of other five year olds next year, and most of those children's parents will have their own expectations for their son's or daughter's first year at school.

Now is the time to get real about what's possible and what's not.

Ask questions, do your research and be ready to share the responsibility for meeting your son's or daughter's needs with teachers. The time you take to establish good lines of communication now will stand you in good stead in the years ahead.

CHAPTER 4

THE BIG SWITCH: PRESCHOOL VS PRIMARY SCHOOL

Kaye's daughter, Chloe, started Kindergarten at a local primary school recently. Chloe endured treatment for a brain tumour at the age of four, and Kaye was naturally worried about how she would cope:

> 'Chloe's been through so much, and I just wanted school to be magical for her. Her little preschool had been so supportive and we felt like everyone there wrapped their arms around us every day. It was a bit of a shock when we went to school and found that, although the teachers cared for Chloe and were very understanding of her needs, the relationship was quite different.'

DEALING WITH LARGER CLASS SIZES

Like Chloe, next year your child will be one of between 15 and 25 very small, very excited little people who will be in the care of one – yes that's right, one – classroom teacher. That's a big change from the nurturing early childhood environment that your sensitive son or daughter may have previously been a part of.

In preschools, the ratio of adults to children is usually about 1:10, but in most Kindergarten, Prep and Reception classrooms, numbers of students are usually higher. Education departments in each state and territory in Australia have their own 'optimal' limits for class sizes in the first year of school, but if your child is going to attend an independent or systemic Catholic school, you may find that these limits do not apply. The record for the biggest Kindergarten class in my local area is 33 students.

Can you imagine being the only adult among that many five year olds?

And you are likely to find that there are a few other differences you and your child will need to adjust to as well. When teachers deal with between 15 and 30 children every day, there are some things that are simply not practical in the classroom. For example, when the children have enjoyed a dance or gymnastics class, it's logistically impossible for the teacher to singlehandedly tie the shoelaces of every single student in the group. So, if your child's uniform policy allows it, do everybody a huge favour: buy school shoes with Velcro tabs next year. (Your child's teacher will be eternally grateful.)

BUILDING RESPONSIBILITY AND INDEPENDENCE

While teachers understand children in their first year of school have a lot to learn, there's a level of independence that they do expect. School is not a place where parents carry their children through the front gate and do things for them that they can do for themselves. Your child's primary school teacher will not hover over your child waiting for an opportunity to step in and save the day. Now is the time for your child to be doing things for themselves and being responsible their own belongings.

Sometimes children with unique needs are used to receiving help from others. Your son or daughter might get a bit of a shock if there's no-one around to lend them a hand next year, so the time to start building self-reliance is now. One way to practise this skill is by giving your son or daughter a backpack to take with them when they go out. It's never too early to place a water bottle, picture book and hat in a bag so that kids have the opportunity to learn to look after their own belongings.

It's inevitable your child will lose things at school. Ask any experienced primary school parent and they will tell you that hats, jumpers and lunchboxes often go AWOL. Expensive musical instruments and school blazers are left on buses, and kids occasionally go home with a classmate's school bag. As you practise with your child this year, you might leave the backpack behind a few times, but this simple strategy is a great way to start building the independence needed for school. Anything you can do now to teach your child to be responsible for themselves and their belongings is a good thing, and will save you a lot of drama in the long run.

WORKING WITH MORE THAN ONE TEACHER

At preschool, your child probably had one teacher and a couple of other staff they knew well. The daily routine was very structured, and your child had comforting routines which were predictable and certain. Next year, your child's classroom will probably have strong routines too, but they will not be the same as the ones your child is used to, and it may take time for your son or daughter to become comfortable.

Another thing to get ready for is the number of teachers who are going to be part of your child's school life. Many parents assume that the classroom teacher is the only adult their child will have regular contact with, and are surprised when their child comes home talking about other teachers they may never have heard of.

Many school starters have contact with five or more teachers each week. In most Australian school systems, classroom teachers spend a couple of hours away from the classroom to write programs, attend meetings and create resources for their students. This 'release from face to face' (RFF) time is part of their timetable, and during their planned weekly absences another teacher will step in to teach your child.

Be prepared for other teachers too. The school librarian, music, science or dance teacher may be part of the class timetable, and there's always a chance that your child will participate in a reading group run by a parent volunteer. The assistant or deputy principal will occasionally pop their head in the door, and as the year progresses, student teachers or prospective parents doing school tours might observe your child's classroom. Every day, a different teacher will be on playground or bus line duty, and don't forget that teachers have days off too. When your child's teacher is attending a professional development day or sick with the flu, casual teachers will step into the breach.

You might be wondering how on earth your child will cope with so much change. Admittedly, it is a lot to get used to, and schools do their best to minimise disruptions during their students' first term at school, but becoming accustomed to the different styles of a variety of adults is a skill you can start helping your child to build now.

Preparing for new voices

Some children with unique needs are used to having one or two trusted educators, and it can be tricky for them to transfer their attention to other people. For example, boys and girls who are anxious sometimes form strong attachments with particular teachers, and kids who have sensory sensitivities can find it hard to cope with adults who have loud voices.

A good way to gently prepare your child for the number of authority figures they will come into contact with next year is to give them lots of learning experiences now:

- In addition to preschool, can you find activities in the community that will give your child the chance to follow instructions and march to the beat of different adults' drums?

- Does your local library offer a weekly story time session that will give your child the chance to become familiar with new adult leaders?

- Would a junior gymnastic, soccer or dance class offer your child an opportunity to follow instructions delivered in new ways?

- Can you find a school readiness class where your child can practise working in a group with other kids?

Anything you do to help your child adjust to having more people in their life will be valuable preparation for next year.

GETTING READY FOR THE PLAYGROUND

The playground is a wonderful place where children explore and develop the relationships that make going to school fun and meaningful. However, for some sensitive children with unique needs, they can also be stressful places.

Play areas

At preschool, teachers often stagger access to the playground so that each group of three and four year olds has exclusive access to it. As a result, your child may have become used to sharing the sandpit, cubby house and tricycles with just 15 or 20 children. At primary school, the story will be very different.

As you well know, schools come in all shapes and sizes. Your child may be part of a tiny school that has fewer than 100 students enrolled, or they could attend a huge metropolitan school with a population of more than 1000 kids. A few years ago, a primary school in my local area had 10 classes in their Kindergarten intake. That's a lot of little bodies to add to a playground.

Before you start to panic about your tiny son or daughter being caught in a stampede of rampaging Year Six boys playing Bullrush, be assured that the school and its teachers will have a plan to help your child integrate into the busy playground. Many schools allocate specific play areas to certain year groups, and it's likely your child will have a designated place in which to play next year.

Buddies

Lots of schools have a buddy system as well. Senior students are matched with school starters so that littlies have an older friend who will look out for them and help them if needed. The children chosen to be part of these peer support initiatives are usually lovely kids who also get a lot out of the leadership opportunities that being a buddy brings. You may find that your child meets their buddy at an orientation day in the year before school starts and will have quite a lot of contact with them in the first few weeks of school.

Playground games

There are many ways you can help your sensitive child to prepare for life in the playground, and one of them is to start teaching your child the rules of common playground games. Many a friendship has been made over a game of handball, and children who have an understanding of the rules of the games that kids play have a distinct advantage when recess and lunchtime roll around.

It's probably been a very long time since you were last in a primary school playground. You may not know where to start, or what games children are playing these days, but don't let that stop you. Young neighbours, nieces or nephews may be able to give you the low down on what's cool and happening at school. You may even be able to enlist their help to teach your school starter some of the games kids are currently playing.

More tips to improve your child's playground prowess can be found on YouTube. Enterprising 12 year olds and their instructional videos explaining the rules of playground games – such as '44 homes', hopscotch and elastics – are a great source of information for unfamiliar parents. When you see how many views their videos have had, you'll soon realise there are thousands of parents around the world who are looking for the same information. (Google can be your best friend in this regard. Just type in 'How to play … ' and you'll get lots of options.)

LEARNING THAT LOSING IS OKAY

Does your child have meltdowns of volcanic proportions when things don't go their way? If so, you're not alone.

Children with unique needs are sometimes easily overwhelmed by feelings like fear and frustration, and when they don't know what to do or how to solve the problem they are facing, a tantrum is often their first and most effective response.

But at school, your explosive child will find that 'chucking a wobbly' is unlikely to get them very far. Teachers, of course, are trained to manage and support children's behaviour, but a five-year-old's peers are not, and so if your child is unable to manage the social and emotional demands of the playground they are unlikely to get much sympathy or forbearance from a pint-sized peer.

Supporting your child's resilience and problem-solving skills is a huge part of raising any child, let alone one who has unique needs. Luckily for us, bookstores and the internet are full of amazing resources on the subject, and so I'm not going to dive into it too deeply here. However, if you are the kind of parent who is still playing backyard soccer and letting your child score all the goals, missing tackles in touch football so that your child makes it to the try line every time, or fudging the results of snakes and ladders so that your child is always a winner, you need to stop. Now.

In this year before school begins, teaching your child how to handle losing is a vital skill, and the best place to learn how to do so is at home in a loving, supportive environment filled with good role models.

As an adult you know that life doesn't always go the way you hope it will. Dealing with disappointment and frustration is sometimes a daily challenge, and you've probably developed mechanisms to deal with big feelings. The problem-solving strategies we use to overcome challenges are learned skills, and for a child to learn these skills they need regular exposure and practice.

If you want your child to have every chance of social success next year, now is the time to start working on these skills. Get professional advice if you need it, but don't underestimate how important this is. Your child's ability to interact with and be accepted by their peers will be one of the biggest factors that affects their education. Don't let being a sore loser be one of the things your child struggles with next year.

Learning with board games

Over the years I've presented many seminars, workshops and keynote speeches on the subject of school readiness. I've spoken to thousands of parents about how to build their child's resilience and problem-solving skills, and introducing board games has been one of the tips I've most commonly given. Board games offer lots of opportunities for children to learn valuable social and cognitive skills, and to learn how to deal with losing. They also build solid family relationships, and are fun too.

There are hundreds of games to choose from, and the games you play will no doubt depend on your child's abilities and interests. I often recommend educational games such as those produced by respected brand Orchard Toys. At my practice in Sydney, I frequently use their 'Spotty Dogs', 'Dotty Dinosaurs' and 'Monster Bingo' games with children who are part of our *Ready Set School* program. These lively board games not only reinforce early language and numeracy concepts, they also give children the chance to practise social skills such as waiting, taking turns and dealing with disappointment.

When my team and I play games with children, we create opportunities to model appropriate behaviours. When something doesn't go our way, we respond with words like, 'Oh dear, that didn't work out for me. Maybe it will next time', or, 'Oh well ... I'll try again when I have my next turn.'

You can do exactly the same thing when you make playing games a part of your family life in the year before your child with unique needs begins school.

Remember, children are like a sponge. They soak up the words and actions of people who influence them, and so when you play games with your child you give them hundreds of opportunities to learn from you. When they see and hear you responding in a positive, solution-focused way, they are more likely to add those responses to their playground patter.

Of course, learning these skills takes time and practice, so don't expect to implement a family board game night on the Friday before school begins and expect that your child will have perfect social skills the following week.

Are there some games you could start playing now? Could loving grandparents, aunties, uncles and friends give board games as birthday or special occasion gifts in the coming year or two? The more games your child plays, the more chances they get to learn to win and lose in a way that the other kids in their class will respect.

CHAPTER 5

10 TOP TIPS TO HELP YOUR CHILD SUCCEED AT SCHOOL

My son has a casual job with one of Australia's major supermarket chains.

During the weeks before Christmas last year he was a checkout champion, serving thousands of last-minute shoppers. He's never worked so hard in his life, and on Christmas Eve, after a long day of price checks and trolleys piled high with hams, he lay on the lounge and said, 'Mum, I couldn't believe it. It's Christmas tomorrow, but we were stocking the shelves with back-to-school stuff today. It's not even January yet!'

'Back to school' is a phenomenon that may engulf you next year as you start to think about important details such as pencil cases and lunchboxes, but before you brave the stationery aisle at Big W, may I share some of my top transition to school tips with you? You don't have to wait until January to implement these strategies, and in fact it's probably better if you don't. The earlier you start preparing, the better.

A school readiness book wouldn't be a school readiness book if it didn't contain practical, commonsense strategies for helping kids get ready for school. This chapter isn't about labels and lunchboxes though. In this chapter you'll find some of the most practical, commonsense ideas my colleagues and I have been sharing for years with thousands of parents who have sensitive children with unique needs.

Don't forget, if you have purchased this book you also have access to my online *School Ready Toolkit*, where you will find free templates and fact sheets, as well as helpful links to other materials for parents and carers.

To download your resources, simply go to my websites www.kids-first.com.au or www.sonjawalker.com.au and use the unique code SchoolReady.

The 10 top tips are:

1. Teach your child to ask for help.
2. Talk about feelings.
3. Play sweet 'n' sour.
4. Have your child's speech and language checked six months before school starts.
5. Create a school story for your child.
6. Use your child's favourite characters.
7. Visit the school informally.
8. Attend orientation days.
9. Get the insights from your child's early educators.
10. Tell the school what it needs to know.

Let's have a look at each of them.

TOP TIP 1: TEACH YOUR CHILD TO ASK FOR HELP

Next year your child will be in a classroom with about 20 or more other children, all vying for the teacher's attention. They might also spend their recess and lunchtimes in playgrounds where there is anywhere between 150 and 800 (or more) other kids also milling around. When your child needs help in these environments, they will need to have the social maturity to be able to ask for it. Trust me, the last thing you need is your Kindy child coming home with wet undies because they weren't game enough to ask if they could go to the toilet.

So what can you do to build this social maturity skill now?

Well, how about teaching your child how to ask for directions when you are out and about? Perhaps they can order from the menu when you eat out at a café, or pay for small items like milk or an ice cream.

These might seem like minor things, and as a parent I know it's sometimes just easier and quicker to read the expression on your child's face and to simply give them what they want. But really, if you are constantly acting as your child's translator and meeting their needs without them ever having to articulate them, you are not helping your child to be independent.

So start now. Teach your child how to ask for what they want (even if you have to whisper in their ear to suggest the words they should say).

TOP TIP 2: TALK ABOUT FEELINGS

Building your child's emotional maturity is an important part of school readiness, and you can do this by helping your son or

daughter to understand their feelings. Sometimes we refer to this as building their 'emotional vocabulary'.

This topic could be the subject of its own book, but put simply, the best way to help your child understand how they and other people feel is to talk about it.

Recognising social cues

Helping your child to recognise the social cues that other people send is part of building their emotional maturity. One way to do this is to talk about the expressions you see on other people's faces. So, for example, you might:

- watch a television program together and talk about how a character in the scene might be feeling

- play a 'mood detective' game when you are out shopping: you could identify a person and say something like, 'That lady over there looks a bit unsure about whether to buy that banana,' or, 'That man pushing the trolleys looks a bit frazzled'.

Small children often don't understand what they are feeling or why they are feeling it, so helping them to label their emotions is a good first step in building awareness of their own emotions and the feelings of others.

Labelling emotions

As much as you can, use 'feelings' words at home so that your child sees you labelling emotions. For example:

- When you're frustrated that you are taking a long time to find a place to park the car at the shopping centre, you might say something like, 'I get a bit annoyed when I waste time looking for a car spot'.

- When you're meeting up with friends, you might say something like, 'I always look forward to seeing Auntie Kate. Getting together with her makes me feel happy.'

Being a 'mirror'

Another way you can do this is by being a bit of a 'mirror' and reflecting your child's feelings back to them. This is important for helping them to recognise both positive and negative feelings.

You might say things like:

- 'I could see that you were so proud when you showed me your painting.'
- 'I know it makes you cranky when your little sister pushes your Lego® over.'
- 'You look a bit upset about that. I can see that your eyes look sad and your face is red.'

Now, your five year old is not going to turn into a sensitive, new-age kid overnight, but research[1] tells us that children who are tuned in to their own feelings and the feelings of the people around them often enjoy greater social and academic success, so it's worth starting to develop this skill in your child now.

TOP TIP 3: PLAY SWEET 'N' SOUR

My favourite game of all time is Sweet 'n' Sour, and if you've ever attended one of my seminars or workshops, you've probably heard me talk about it. Even today, my family plays it at dinnertime and

---

1   Wilson, KR, Havighurst, SS and Harley, AE (2012). 'Tuning in to Kids: An effectiveness trial of a parenting program targeting emotion socialization of preschoolers'. *Journal of Family Psychology*, 26.1, 56–65.

the teenagers who frequently visit my place to devour a gourmet meal cooked by my husband are always keen to play too.

Sweet 'n' Sour is quite simple. Everyone at the table talks about the 'sweetest' thing that happened during their day, and they also share the 'sourest' thing that occurred. Now, as a grown up you may need to 'filter' your sweet and sour anecdotes, but this lovely mealtime routine has lots of benefits to offer to your child and family.

When each child has their moment to share their experiences with the people they love, they get the opportunity to talk about things they felt strongly about that day. Extroverted children who dominate dinnertime conversation have to make way for quieter siblings, and sensitive children who don't like to have the spotlight become more comfortable speaking up. And when children hear parents talking about the joys and challenges of their day, they learn that everyone has ups and downs. This perspective is important as we model problem solving and resilience to our children.

Sweet 'n' Sour is also a terrific way to gauge how your child is going at preschool or school. If the same names keep popping up in your child's recounts of the day, this may indicate that there is a fledgling friendship forming and an invitation for a playdate might be in order. Equally, if something (or someone) is bothering your child on a regular basis, this might provide an opportunity for you to find out more from teachers about what is happening in the classroom or playground.

Later in this book, you'll read more about the importance of building a solid relationship with your child. After all, when your child is 15 and it's 2.00 am, you want them to feel connected enough to you for them to call and say, 'I need to leave. Can you come and pick me up?' Building the foundations for that kind of trusting relationship starts now, and playing Sweet 'n' Sour is a great way to begin.

TOP TIP 4: HAVE YOUR CHILD'S SPEECH AND LANGUAGE CHECKED SIX MONTHS BEFORE SCHOOL STARTS

As a parent, I'm sure I don't have to convince you of the important role your child's communication skills will play when they head off to school. We all know that children need to be able to speak to make friends. We also know that children need to be able to understand what is said to them so that they can learn.

Research tells us your child's speech and language skills are the single most powerful and sensitive indicator of his or her development.[2] In other words, what your child is able to say, explain and understand *now* is a really good guide to how he or she will cope in a formal schooling environment next year.

As a teacher who leads a children's health team you'd probably expect me to tell you this, but according to every principal, preschool director and primary school teacher I have interviewed for this book, good communication skills are fundamental if your child is going to be able to take an active part in family, school and social life.

Did you know that Australian studies have revealed that up to one in six Australian preschoolers has a speech or language delay?[3] This is quite an alarming statistic, because it means that up to 15 per cent of preschoolers struggle with the skills they need to enjoy school and be successful in their learning.

---

2   Taylor, CL and Zubrick, S (2009). 'Predicting Children's Speech, Language and Reading Impairment Over Time', *International Journal of Speech-Language Pathology*, 11(5): 341–3.
3   McLeod S, Harrison LJ (2009). 'Epidemiology of Speech and Language Impairment in a Nationally Representative Sample of 4- to 5-year-old Children', *Journal of Speech, Language, and Hearing Research*, 52(5):1213–29.

Typically, the kinds of problems these children have include issues with:

- attention and listening
- receptive language: understanding ideas, concepts, instructions and questions
- expressive language: the ability to express their ideas in words and sentences
- speech: the ability to articulate sounds and words correctly
- social communication: appropriate interaction skills when playing and learning.

You might be tempted to think, *well, if my child's speech or language is delayed they are in good company – there'll be three other kids in their Kindy class who are just like them.*

You'd also be forgiven for believing that your child will grow out of any issues they have now. And if all the stars align, they just might.

But are you prepared to take that risk?

As alarming as the statistics are, they are, unfortunately, also pretty accurate. Put simply, children with speech or language difficulties are at a greater risk of having literacy difficulties. In fact, influential international research has revealed that 41 per cent to 75 per cent of children whose early language delays are not addressed when they are little continue to show reading problems at the age of eight.[4]

At Kids First, my speech pathologist colleagues regularly work with school-aged children who are an example of this statistic. Typically they are aged between six and nine, and despite everything their parents and teachers have done to support their literacy, they

---

[4] Law J, Boyle J, Harris F, Harkness A, Nye C (1998). 'Screening for Primary Speech and Language Delay: A systematic review of the literature,' *International Journal of Language & Communication Disorders*, 33 Suppl: 21-3.

struggle with reading and spelling until a speech pathologist uncovers underlying speech and language issues that are contributing to their problems. Once those problems are identified and customised support is put in place, they make progress, but often it takes a while to catch up to where their classmates are at.

I'd hate your child to struggle next year, and so I encourage you to have your child's hearing, speech and language checked at least six months before school starts. If you get nothing more than peace of mind from your visits to an audiologist and speech pathologist, that's great. If it turns out that there are a few things you need to work on with your child, you'll have time to address them before January so your son or daughter has the best chance possible to play and learn like the other kids in their class.

> **SCHOOL READY TOOLKIT**
>
> You'll find a *School Ready Speech and Language Skills Checklist* in my School Ready Toolkit. Go to www.kids-first.com.au or www.sonjawalker.com.au and use the unique code SchoolReady to download your free copy.

TOP TIP 5: CREATE A SCHOOL STORY FOR YOUR CHILD

School stories are a fantastic way to help your sensitive child understand what to expect when they go to school. Inspired by the idea of a 'Social Story'[5] developed by teacher Carol Gray, you can make and print a customised school story for your child so they become familiar with the people and places who will be part of their life when they go to school next year.

---

5   Gray, C (2000). *The New Social Story Book: Illustrated edition*. Arlington, TX: Future Horizons.

You might be surprised at how easy it is to create a school story for your child. If your phone has a camera and you have a computer and printer at home, you have all you need. Local libraries and retail giants like Officeworks can also help you out with printing if need be.

What to include in your child's school story

While it might not be possible yet for the school to confirm who next year's teacher will be, there are still lots of specific pictures and words that can be part of your child's school story.

Here are some photo ideas to get you started:

- an internal shot of the classroom that your child might be in next year
- the area outside the classroom where children leave their school bags
- the spot in the playground where your child will sit to eat lunch
- the boys' and girls' toilets (if you have a son, a photo of the urinals might be a useful addition too)
- the COLA (school speak for 'covered outdoor learning area')
- play equipment such as cubby houses and climbing frames
- the canteen
- the drop-off and pick-up area in the playground or carpark
- the front office.

As I've already mentioned, the people in the front office secretly run the school, so a happy photo of their friendly faces is always a good addition to your child's school story because they are likely to be your child's first port of call when something goes wrong in the playground.

Get permission from the school

When preparing your child's school story, it's important to consider privacy, child protection and other school protocols. A stranger wandering around the school with a camera is likely to cause concern, so if you would like to take photos at your child's prospective school, make sure you have the school's permission to do so. In this era of social media, it's only reasonable for teachers to know why you want to take photos and what you're planning to do with them. If the school is okay with your school story idea, you might find that popping in after school hours is the best time to take photos. This will ensure you don't disrupt classes or accidentally record images of other people's children.

Once you have the photos you need, simply insert them into the template you will find in the *School Ready Toolkit* that comes with this book, print it out and start enjoying it with your child.

You might be surprised by how frequently your child refers to their school story in the months before school begins. It's a great way to start conversations, build familiarity and give confidence so that your sensitive child feels ready for their next adventure at school.

> **SCHOOL READY TOOLKIT**
>
> You'll find a *School Story Template* in my School Ready Toolkit. Go to www.kids-first.com.au or www.sonjawalker.com.au and use the unique code SchoolReady to download your free copy.

TOP TIP 6: USE YOUR CHILD'S FAVOURITE CHARACTERS

Did you know that Thomas the Tank Engine has been to school? I didn't either, but sure enough, just like Maisie and Dora the Explorer, according to the children's picture book which tells the story of his first day at 'big school', he has.

For many sensitive children, the idea of doing something new is a bit confronting. Going to school for the first time brings a lot of change all at once, and it's fairly natural for your child to feel a bit anxious in the months leading up to their first day.

Using the experiences of trusted characters is one way to help your child overcome their uncertainty. 'Going to school' books normalise the concept of starting school. They often cover some of the common experiences that children have in the lead up to their transition from preschool, including fears like worrying about being left behind or getting lost. Visualising these concepts helps children to understand that other children might be a bit nervous too.

Reading these kinds of books with your child will give you opportunities to talk to them about the situations they might encounter next year. These conversations are really valuable, and by getting worries out into the open you are giving your child the chance to process and problem solve before their jitters get the better of them.

So, does your child have a favourite character, and has that character been to school? Your local library might have an extensive collection of books that you could borrow. Going-to-school books also make great gifts, so if doting relatives are looking for something special to give your child, these kinds of stories are a good option.

> **SCHOOL READY TOOLKIT**
>
> You'll find *Best Books for School Starters* in my School Ready Toolkit. Go to www.kids-first.com.au or www.sonjawalker.com.au and use the unique code SchoolReady to download your free copy.

TOP TIP 7: VISIT THE SCHOOL INFORMALLY

The months leading up to your child's transition to school are the perfect time to get to know their new environment, but how can you do that when they are at preschool and you are busy at home or work? The answer is by taking opportunities to visit the school informally.

Fourth term is often a busy time for fetes, fairs, art shows and other events that bring school communities together. Not only is the weather a bit more predictable in Spring, but it's usually taken all year for the school community and its Parents and Citizens' Association (P & C) to organise the event, so the timing couldn't be more perfect for you and your child.

There's a lot of value in giving your child simple opportunities to be in their new environment when no-one is expecting anything of them. You can use informal visits to check the school out and build your child's familiarity with its playgrounds and classrooms, as well as the teachers and other people they will meet next year.

Most primary schools have a weekly assembly, and these are another way to show your child what school is all about. You'll need the school's permission to attend, of course, but you might find that assemblies offer your child reassuring chances to see the school in action before term one begins.

TOP TIP 8: ATTEND ORIENTATION DAYS

For your sensitive child, attending orientation days is very important, and I encourage you to make them a priority in your calendar. Your child's new school is likely to offer at least one designated orientation day when you and your child are invited to visit the school for a morning. Typically, your child will spend time in the school's Kindergarten classrooms, engage in group activities, and perhaps meet children in Year Five who could be their 'buddies' next year. Many schools offer sessions for parents while the children are occupied, and this can be a good way to learn more about the school and meet other families. Some schools have extensive transition programs that run over several weeks to give new students and their parents the opportunity to get to know the school.

Orientation days are helpful for a number of reasons. Obviously, they give your child a chance to meet prospective classmates and be in the classroom environment that they will be part of next year. But perhaps less obviously, they give you the opportunity to see how your child interacts and copes with new people and places too.

Despite what you might have heard, teachers typically don't use orientation days for the purpose of educational assessments. What they do use them for, however, is to get a general idea of group dynamics.

Some kids need more than just one orientation day, and you might find that the school is open to organising extra visits for you and your child. In the term before he started school, my son joined the Kindergarten class for a couple of hours each fortnight and the familiarity it gave him made a world of difference when school began the following year.

Try to remember, though, that orientation day is not the day to ambush teachers or the principal and have a deep and meaningful conversation about your child's needs. There could be as many as 100 other parents and children visiting on the same day, and you will not get the attention or support of staff if you choose the wrong time and place to discuss these kinds of private matters.

If you think your child is going to need more support than the orientation schedule provides for, make an appointment to chat with staff on another day when things aren't quite so hectic. You'll find that your sensitivity is appreciated, and your relationship with the school will get off to a much better start.

TOP TIP 9: GET INSIGHTS FROM YOUR CHILD'S EARLY EDUCATORS

There is one group of people whose value and expertise is often overlooked when parents start to think about preparing their child for school, and that's early childhood educators.

Early childhood educators who have spent time with your son or daughter can offer a perspective that is very different to yours. While you see your child through the lens of your family, they see your child in the context of a group of similarly aged peers. They have objective and informed insights into your child's social, emotional, physical and learning skills which might not be visible to you.

In years past, staff who worked in preschools and daycare centres have been unfairly labelled as 'glorified babysitters', and it's time to challenge that misconception.

Twenty-first-century early childhood educators are tertiary-educated professionals with extensive training and knowledge of child development. They are passionate about helping children make the best possible start to life, and are keen to support you as you raise your child. Early childhood centres are led by qualified teachers who

have a wealth of experience to share. While your family might be embarking on the transition to school for the first time, your child's preschool teachers have probably walked this path with hundreds of other families.

If your child has unique needs, it's likely that you have had more than a few conversations with your son's or daughter's early childhood educators this year. They may not have been easy, but believe me when I tell you that keeping these lines of communication open is important.

No early childhood educator wants to let parents know their child is struggling. They don't take pleasure in telling you that your child is finding something difficult, and they don't enjoy sharing information that you might find worrying. However, if your child's preschool teacher taps you on the shoulder and invites you to come by for a chat, I encourage you to see this as an opportunity to get advice, information and resources from a professional who takes their responsibility to you and your child very seriously.

It might seem easier for your child's preschool teachers not to say anything to you about your child's challenges. After all, your child is going to school next year and maybe it will all turn out well in the end. But good early childhood educators don't have this attitude. They understand the importance of early intervention, and they are committed to giving you the opportunity to make informed choices for your child.

So, in these months before school starts, I encourage you to seek out and act upon the advice you receive from your child's preschool teachers. Make good use of their expertise and take advantage of their practical, real-life understanding of your child's skills and abilities. The knowledge you gain and the help they can give could be invaluable in January.

TOP TIP 10: TELL THE SCHOOL WHAT IT NEEDS TO KNOW

The line between your family's privacy and the things schools need to know can sometimes be a fine one. Social stigma is a terrible thing, and if you and your child have been on the receiving end of others' harsh judgements in the past, it's understandable that trusting strangers with intensely personal information about your child might be difficult.

Having said that, teachers and schools can't help your child if they don't have the information they need to give your son or daughter the assistance you are expecting from them.

You could be forgiven for assuming that, because primary school teachers have helped so many little kids start school, your child's teachers will automatically know what to do and how to cater for your child's unique needs next year. But if the principal doesn't know that your child suffers with anxiety or is diagnosed with autism or ADHD, how can he or she allocate extra teacher resources to the classroom or playground to support your child?

If they don't know that your child has experienced a bereavement, family breakup or other difficult domestic situations, how will the school counsellor know that they might need to reach out to you to see if there is an extra support that your child needs?

If your child is gifted, how can the school offer extension or acceleration classes if you haven't provided them with documentation outlining your child's learning differences? Equally, if your child has identified learning, language or sensory difficulties, how can the Learning Support Teacher make sure your child is included in his or her timetable if you are not forthcoming with information about your child's unique needs before school begins?

It's hard to talk to strangers about the things that make our children vulnerable. I've lost count of how many times I've cried in meetings with teachers, principals and other professionals, and I still choke up when I think or talk about the challenges my son has faced.

As parents, we get emotional. It's natural and normal to get upset when you have to explain the hurts your child has, and we worry that we might appear weak, or that the school might get the wrong idea about us too. But the bottom line is that, if we don't tell the school what is going on for our child, we really don't have the right to expect that they will work it out for themselves. By not telling teachers about your child's unique needs, you actually make it harder for them to do their jobs. Keeping quiet about challenges means that your child might struggle needlessly, or be placed in situations that will lead to meltdowns and misunderstandings.

If you have a gifted child, don't you want him or her to have the teacher who has a special interest in this area of education?

If you have a child with a disability, don't you want the school to apply for funding or extra resources so that they are in place on day one?

If your child has had a tough couple of years, don't you want your son or daughter to have access to extra support and understanding?

If your child has unique needs, be brave and have the conversation. Your sensitive child does not have to wear a label for all to see, and you can request that this information be kept confidential, but teachers value your candour and your trust in them.

If you start your relationship with your child's school in an open and honest way, you have the best chance of building a collaborative partnership that is in everyone's interest, including your child's.

* * *

There's a lot to think about, isn't there? If your 'to do' list has doubled in size after reading all of the advice shared in this chapter, just remember that none of these steps need to be taken at the same time. It's perfectly natural to feel a bit overwhelmed by the decisions you're making and the things you feel you need to do before school starts next year, but don't forget to ask for help if you need it.

Every year your child's current early educators help children to transition to school, and every year teachers at your child's new primary school do exactly the same thing. If you have questions, ask them early enough so you can act on the answers. If you are feeling calm and certain about the choices you've made, your child will pick up on your confidence and will be more likely to look forward to the adventures that 'big school' will bring.

CHAPTER 6

AT WHAT AGE SHOULD MY CHILD START SCHOOL?

'The New South Wales Department of Education told us that the boys could start school because they turned five in February, which was well before the cut-off date of 31 July. With triplets, we had to make choices for three children, not just one, so we based all our planning on sending them to school at the age of five. Then we found out there would be six year olds in the class because the rules said that children must be enrolled by their sixth birthday. We discovered that other parents were holding their kids back so that they would be older when they started school. It was quite stressful. Just when we thought we knew what we were doing, we started questioning the decisions we'd made. If we'd sent them to school at the age of five they might have been more than a year younger than many of their peers. In the end, we chose to hold them back, but it wasn't an easy decision and it meant we had to find a way to pay for preschool for all three of them for another year.'

Rachel, mother of Bailey, Jasper and Oliver

Life has certainly been busy for Rachel since her triplets Bailey, Jasper and Ollie were born, and getting all three boys ready to start school was a project that started quite early for Sydney-based Rachel and her husband Matt.

All around Australia, parents just like Rachel and Matt are worried about whether now is the right time to be sending their child to school. You might be one of them.

STARTING AGES ACROSS THE COUNTRY

The fact that each state has its own rules about how old kids need to be to start school doesn't help. The wide age range for enrolments often means that it's possible for some children in the class to be more than 12 months younger than their classmates, and this raises all kinds of issues for parents of children with unique needs. While a uniform approach to school starting ages around the country might seem sensible, no consensus has yet been reached, so at the time of writing, children in each state must have turned five on or before the following cut-off dates to be able to start school.

State or Territory	Cut-off date
Tasmania	1 January
Victoria and ACT	30 April
South Australia	1 May
Queensland, Western Australia and Northern Territory	30 June
New South Wales	31 July

At what age should my child start school?

THERE IS MUCH MORE TO SCHOOL READINESS THAN CHRONOLOGICAL AGE

Even though the Australian Primary Principals Association has said it believes the cut-off should be turning five by the end of term one, the bottom line is that there is much more to school readiness than chronological age.

One of my most memorable students is a little boy called Kyle who started school at the age of four years and nine months. Chronological age didn't matter for Kyle. He celebrated his fifth birthday in May, and was a bright and extroverted little boy who was the middle child in a family of seven children. Despite being up to 15 months younger than some of his peers, Kyle had the social, emotional and learning skills he needed to start school successfully, and that's just what he did. Fast forward a few years and Kyle was elected captain at his primary school, and is now enjoying life as a high schooler.

Is now the right time?

If your child with unique needs is at the younger end of the age range, it's perfectly understandable to worry about what this might mean for your child's education and future.

Psychologist and education academic Dr Amanda Mergler and her colleague Professor Susan Walker recently conducted a study that followed more than 220,000 Australian primary schoolers through their transitions to school.[6] When I caught up with Dr Mergler, she told me that the research confirmed what parents, teachers and other professionals have known for some time: children's chronological age is a big consideration for many parents, and the number

---

6   Mergler, A and Walker, S (2017). "'This is Possibly THE Hardest Decision a Parent Has to Make.' Deciding When Your Child is Ready to Start Prep', *Australasian Journal of Early Childhood*, Volume 42, Number 2.

of Australian mums and dads who are delaying their child's start to school is growing.

Her research indicated that parents whose children have birthdays that fall near cut-off dates are particularly anxious about the choices they make for their kids. It also revealed that families who have sons at the younger end of their cohort are the ones most likely to be thinking about delaying their child's start to school.

You might be one of these parents.

Not only are you wondering whether your child has the social, emotional and developmental skills to meet the demands of a Kindergarten classroom, but you also might be thinking about how your son or daughter will cope later in their school lives if issues such as peer pressure, drinking, relationships and the rigours of senior study pop up during the final years of school. It's perfectly reasonable to want to give your child the very best chance to have a successful start to school. No parent wants their child to be behind the eight ball before they begin, and your desire to not disadvantage your child with a poor choice is natural.

If your child's birthday falls right in the middle of the age bracket for school transition, then by virtue of its cut-off dates, your local Department of Education may have made the decision for you. However, if you have options about the timing of your child's transition from preschool to school, try to consider this choice as a great opportunity for your son or daughter.

Remember, school readiness for any child, and especially those with unique needs, is about more than how old they are. Instead of worrying about whether your child's age will set them apart from the rest of the kids in their class, think instead about the skills your child has and whether they have the social and emotional maturity to use them.

Six key skills that indicate school readiness

If you're agonising over whether your child's age is going to be a major factor in their school success, you're probably posing hypothetical questions that are impossible to answer right now.

Being happy and successful at school usually doesn't depend solely on how old a child is. While social and emotional maturity do, of course, play a big part in how kids cope with the demands of the classroom and playground, there are some other skills that kids really do need to succeed in a Kindergarten classroom. Turning your attention to them is probably a better use of your energy right now.

Instead of making your school transition decisions on the basis of whether your child is older or younger than the other kids in their class, perhaps it would be more helpful to think about how well your child is able to do the things that Kindy kids need to be able to do in their first year at school. Here's six key skills that are more important than age:

1   *The ability to pay attention for at least 10 minutes.*

    Next year, your child will be constantly introduced to new ideas, rules and skills, so being able to focus on a task will be important in the classroom and in the playground. If your son or daughter is one of the many kids who is easily distracted or finds it hard to concentrate on one activity at a time, now is the time to find ways to support their ability to filter unimportant sights, sounds and information out. At home, try giving your child deadlines for completing tasks so they learn to plan their time. You could use the timer on the oven, or alternatively use one of the many visual tools that teachers and therapists use to support children with attentional issues. At Kids First Children's Services, we use special clocks called 'Time Timers' that show children how long they have left to finish what they are doing. Time Timers also come as an

app, and are a handy tool for parents. If you are worried about your child's attention skills, think about having them checked by an occupational therapist or speech pathologist too. Sometimes, concentration challenges are caused by underlying communication or core strength issues which, when discovered early enough, can be addressed before your child heads off to school.

2   *The ability to interact with other children positively and with minimal conflict.*

School is a very social place, and next year your child will spend hours and hours in the company of other kids. Typically, Kindergarten teachers arrange the desks in their classrooms so that children work in small groups, and of course the playground will also require your child to negotiate with other kids as they play, so your child will be expected to interact with classmates all day long. For some children, dealing with the unpredictability of their peers is tricky. If your child is an only child, they might not have had as much contact with other kids, or if your child is gifted, their interests could differ from those of classmates. If you have an anxious child, interacting with other little humans could be unsettling too. Many children need practice to socialise successfully, so in the coming months, try to give your child opportunities to be in the company of other children. Some ideas include attending story time at your local library, a junior sport, dance or gymnastics class, or even regular playdates with the children of friends and family. Practise at home too, with games in which you and your child take turns to role-play social situations.

3   *The capacity to comply with routines and structured activities.*

Teachers create classroom routines to help children learn, so helping your child get used to the structure that teachers will add to their day is an important school readiness skill.

Therapists and educators often use visual schedules to support children's understanding of what comes next, and this could be a helpful technique for you to use at home too. Simple storyboards containing pictures of the day's activities are easy to create, and with the help of a bit of Blu Tack™, you can compile a DIY visual schedule for your child that could make life a lot easier for them and you. If you're on the go and want to take your visual schedules with you, there are quite a few apps on the market that could be helpful too. New apps are being developed all the time, but resources such as the Visual Schedule Planner or the First Then Visual Schedule are popular and could be a good starting point for you and your child.

4   *The ability to follow simple, clear instructions.*

Being able to march to the beat of someone else's drum is a challenge for some little kids, and so if your child has an independent spirit and finds it hard to comply with instructions, now is the time to get some practice in. A good first step is to have your child's hearing checked, especially if they have been prone to lots of colds and ear infections during their preschool years.

If hearing is not an issue and following instructions is a problem for your child, support your child's understanding by always ensuring you have eye contact with them before you ask them to do something for you. The visual schedules mentioned above could also be useful – I know plenty of families who have them placed all over the house so their children have a better chance of remembering the things they need to do. When my son was little, I had a visual schedule posted in the bathroom when he was learning all the steps involved in going to the loo! If you're tired of reminding your kids to flush and wash their hands, this is a technique you could try too, as you build your child's ability to follow instructions.

5   *The capacity to communicate effectively with others.*

Being able to understand and be understood is a critical school readiness skill, and without it your child is likely to find it challenging to meet the social and learning demands of the classroom and playground. According to Speech Pathology Australia, the speech of a typical five year old should be able to be understood by unfamiliar adults most of the time.[7] Even though your school starter might still have trouble saying sounds like 's', 'r', 'l' and 'th', having conversations and telling simple stories that have a beginning, middle and end should come naturally to them by the time school begins. If your child is already speaking easily, is understanding everything that is said to them, and is able to engage confidently in conversation with adults and peers, that's great! If you have any niggling worries, or if it's obvious that your child isn't able to speak and listen as their peers do, take the time to have your child checked by a speech pathologist now. There may be nothing to be concerned about, but it's better to know and be able to take action before term one starts, than to let a problem escalate and interfere with your child's confidence and success next year.

6   *Self-reliance when managing self-care tasks such as asking for help or using a toilet independently.*

If you have a sensitive child who has unique needs, you may have become used to being your son's or daughter's 'helper'. This is understandable because day-to-day life is often easier for kids when adults take the lead, and it can be less stressful for parents too because things get done more quickly and with less drama. Unfortunately, you won't be there to help your child every step of the way next year, and so now is the time to build your child's ability to recognise their own needs and

---

7   Speech Pathology Australia 2016, 'The Sound of Speech: Preschool and school aged children', accessed 12 January 2018, http://www.speechpathologyaustralia.org.au.

At what age should my child start school?

act upon them. As you start to prepare your child for school, a simple question to ask yourself is, 'What is the least I can do to do help my child to succeed?' The more often you step back and allow your child to problem solve for themselves, the better equipped your child will be when school begins.

In my seminars, workshops and private practice work, I've advised thousands of parents to think about these things in the year before their child starts school. The earlier you do it, the better equipped you and your sensitive child will be when January rolls around.

* * *

The time to send your child to school is when they are ready to thrive, and not just cope.

Is your child ready to thrive?

If your answer is 'not yet', don't panic. You still have time.

PART II

DEVELOPING GREAT RELATIONSHIPS WITH TEACHERS AND OTHER PARENTS

'When children are very little, it takes a lot to hand them over to strangers. Early educators are usually the first people outside the family that children are entrusted to and sometimes we get quite close to families. When parents don't have a local support network of family and friends, they tend to build very strong bonds with us, so when it comes time to say goodbye, leaving preschool can be almost as difficult for the parent as it is for the child. The tissue box in my office always gets a good workout in the months before school starts because it's such an emotional time for everyone.'

Michele, preschool director

Michele is one of the finest early childhood educators I've ever met. After more than 30 years working with other people's children, and as the parent of a child with unique needs herself, she cares deeply about families and knows how challenging it can be to raise kids in this day and age.

Your child may have been lucky enough to have an early childhood educator just like Michele. You may have come to depend on teachers or trusted therapists who have helped you through some tough times, and you may even regard them as part of your extended family. It's perfectly normal to feel a little reluctant about leaving the comfortable relationships you and your child have enjoyed in recent years, and to wonder how you will manage without their regular support and encouragement.

When my son left his early intervention program in 2005, I cried like a baby. We were all very fond of the staff, and I depended heavily on them for support and guidance. Making the break was hard, so if you're lying awake at night worrying about what's going to happen at school next year, you are not alone.

In the months before school begins, it's natural to wonder if your child is really ready for school, and for parents like you and me there are lots of 'what ifs'.

We worry that we haven't done enough and whether the choices we've made will turn out to be mistakes.

We worry that we will be misunderstood and that our children will be harshly judged by their teachers, peers and other parents.

We worry that we won't have the skills or knowledge to be good advocates for our kids, and we worry that our children will suffer as a result.

Our secret worries are rarely talked about at the preschool gate, and they're certainly not often covered in the many school readiness books and online articles that we look to for answers.

So let's change that.

Let's talk about the 'what ifs' and what you can do to achieve peace of mind as your child with unique needs starts school.

CHAPTER 7

CREATING UNDERSTANDING AT SCHOOL

> 'Leo has a good heart and wants to be friends with everyone, but sometimes he doesn't know when to stop. When he was diagnosed with ADHD last year, one teacher told me that she didn't believe in the condition and that he just needed better parenting and more boundaries. I went home and cried.'
>
> *Jenny, Leo's mum*

Jenny's son, Leo, is an active boy who is always on the go. Most four year olds find it hard to sit still for any length of time, but Leo really struggles to stay in one spot, wait or take turns.

Leo's preschool years weren't exactly smooth sailing for Jenny, and in fact he was asked to leave two early childhood centres because other parents complained about his boisterous behaviour. The experience left Jenny feeling anxious about teachers and worried about how Leo might be perceived when he started school.

If you're lying awake at night worrying that your sensitive child's needs aren't going to be understood, you're not alone. I'd hazard a guess that most parents of kids with unique needs have felt exactly as you do. So, how can you guarantee the teachers, parents and children that your child will join at school next year will understand what life is like for you and your child?

Well, the simple answer is, you can't.

While it's likely that you'll meet some people who are very sympathetic and supportive when your child starts school, there is also a pretty good chance that, over the next few years, you'll meet others who aren't. One of the hardest things in the world is dealing with people who just don't get it. They're everywhere. In workplaces. In restaurants and cafés. In supermarkets, and sadly, even in schools.

And that won't necessarily be because they don't care or are nasty people. It just might be that their ability to see things from your perspective is limited by their own experiences. Or it might be because you haven't communicated the information they need to understand your child as well as you could have.

UNDERSTANDING IS A TWO-WAY STREET

Every teacher brings a set of individual personal and professional experiences to their classroom. Every principal is constrained by policies and procedures they must follow. Every parent has values and ideas about how they want to raise their children, and because we are all different, the way other people see things might be different from the way you do. That's why it's important to have realistic expectations about how much teachers will know and understand when they meet your child for the first time next year.

For example, I don't know what it's like to have twins or triplets, but perhaps you do.

And I don't know what it's like to have a gifted child, but maybe you live with one every day.

I don't know what it's like to raise a child on my own, but perhaps being a single parent is your reality.

And I don't know what it's like to live in a community where my first language is not widely spoken, but if you grew up overseas this could be a constant challenge for you.

As a teacher who hasn't walked in your shoes or lived with your child, I can appreciate the challenges you face every day, but until you tell me what they are, I can't truly understand them.

Often, we expect a lot from the people at our child's school. We expect that, because we've written a sentence or two on an enrolment form, or had a brief conversation on open day, that they will remember what we have told them. We expect that, because they are teachers, they will know exactly what accommodations our child might need in the classroom or playground when they arrive at school.

But having this expectation is probably a bit unrealistic.

Next year, people will need to get to know you and your child before they can really understand the things that make your family unique. This takes time and effort, on both parts.

NOW *THAT'S* A KNIFE

Here's a little story that demonstrates how important it is to have understanding and a good relationship with teachers at your child's school.

It was a lovely Spring day in late November when my son found himself in a spot of bother.

You see, he accidentally took a knife to school.

And as Crocodile Dundee might have described it, it wasn't just any knife. It was a great big carving knife that might have held pride of place in Gordon Ramsay's kitchen.

When he found it in his backpack, my son did what only a child of mine could do. He wondered how it had got there, and because he knew he hadn't put it there, simply carried on with his day.

Did he go to the front office and report it? No.

Did he call his mum to ask what he should do? No.

The knife's existence only came to light when a teacher almost tripped over his bag, and he matter-of-factly warned her that his backpack contained a knife. The teacher did what every good teacher would do when faced with a kid who has told her he has a knife in his bag. She sent my son, and his accidental knife, to the Deputy Principal.

And this is where understanding kicked in.

You see, the Deputy Principal knew my son, and she knew me.

I swear that on that day, when things could have gone pear-shaped so quickly, the countless conversations, P & C and School Council meetings, trivia nights and general chats I'd had with her and her colleagues over the years came into play. The Deputy Principal hadn't only met me once a year at parent–teacher nights. She'd met me many, many times in other contexts. She'd laughed with me in light-hearted moments as we chatted about family holidays and the adventures of her new grandchildren. She had even listened with interest when I confided that I was going to write a book.

She knew about my son's struggles, and she knew that I could be a bit of a 'lioness' when it came to my boy. She also knew about my background as a teacher and what I do for a living now. She knew me as a *person*, not just as another school parent who only shows up when things go wrong – and that made all the difference.

On that day, that wonderful teacher used her understanding of my son to manage the position he found himself in with sensitivity and commonsense. Instead of placing the school into lockdown and suspending him on the spot, she considered the merits and circumstances of the situation. She spoke to him and saw that he was as mystified about the origins of the knife as she was. Because she knew me, she sent him back to class, and picked up the phone. Fortunately, the person she called was me.

The opportunity she gave me to talk to my son about what was going on was a gift. A gift of time to sort it out. An opportunity to find out if there was something else going on, and a chance to put my son's wellbeing before due process.

You can imagine that the chat his dad and I had with him at home that afternoon was a pretty serious one. Was he feeling overwhelmed? Was he being bullied? What had he planned to do with the knife? What on earth had he been thinking?

As my son sat there and proclaimed his innocence, I produced the photo of the knife the Deputy Principal had sent me, and that's when the penny dropped for my husband – who recognised it straight away.

'That's *my* knife … ' he said. 'When we were leaving Lake Crackenback, I did a last check of the kitchen and realised I'd almost left it behind in the top drawer. You were putting the bags in the car and I knew we had to get going, so I just put it into the bottom of the …'

And there was a pause.

'Backpack?' offered my son. 'Dad! Really?'

The mystery was solved, and more importantly, the Deputy Principal and her equally sensible boss believed the admittedly far-fetched but absolutely true story we told them.

No-one was suspended, but valuable lessons were learned.

A certain boy learned how lucky he was to have a great teacher who 'got it'.

His dad learned to be more careful with his kitchen utensils.

And his mum learned that the time and effort she'd put in to being involved in her child's school had not been wasted … and that she'd never rush her husband to pack the car again.

Understanding takes time

Can you spot the moral in this story?

As a parent who is about to embark on a new relationship with your child's first school, I encourage you to be as involved as possible in your child's education. The positives that come when parents and teachers get to know one another as people are immeasurable, and you will never fully appreciate how important your relationships at school are until you encounter a bump in the road and have to find a way to get over it.

SHARE THE GOOD STUFF TOO

If you are going to be the kind of parent whose contact with the school is confined to epic 1000-word emails, after-school teacher ambushes and weekly phone calls to the principal, you're unlikely to build much rapport with the school and its staff.

But, if you are the kind of parent who puts their hand up to help in the classroom, attends P & C meetings every six weeks, or gives up a morning for a once-a-term working bee, you will find that, over time, you will have many informal opportunities to get to know teachers (and other parents).

And while you're doing that, they're getting to know you too.

But there's also more to building relationships than just showing up to events. Letting teachers know and acknowledging when things are going well is just as important as keeping them in the loop when your sensitive child is struggling. Parents who recognise the extra effort staff make and don't leave it until the end of the year to say thank you are really appreciated by hard-working educators. So next year, if you have five minutes to spare, it might be nice to send an email, card or quick note to your child's teacher to share some good news.

Positive words and actions help to build positive relationships, and positive relationships between parents and teachers build better outcomes for kids.

THINGS WILL BE DIFFERENT

As you head off to 'big school' with your child, try to remember that the relationship you build with your child's primary school teachers may not be like the close, first-name-basis bonds you previously enjoyed with their early childhood educators. Next year, you may find that after-school staff meetings, extracurricular coaching responsibilities and even their private role as parents to their own children might mean your child's teacher can't stop to chat with you for ten minutes every day.

Their apparent reluctance to spontaneously stay until 3.45 pm to talk with you about your child's unique needs is unlikely to be the result of a lack of interest, and if you interpret it that way, you will miss the point. Most teachers are more than happy to organise a time to talk with you about important matters. When they meet

with you, they want to be able to prepare for your conversation by gathering resources so they can answer your questions thoroughly and address your concerns.

Ambushing them on the doorstep of the classroom is not the way to build understanding or cooperation, so if you show that you respect their time by making an appointment that's mutually convenient, you will go a long way to building a positive partnership.

SCHOOL IS NEW FOR YOU TOO

Like Jenny, you may have had discouraging experiences with teachers in the past, or you might have heard horror stories from other parents about how schools have handled their children with unique needs.

It's natural to worry that your child might be misunderstood at school, but remember, the future is not always determined by the past.

If you are feeling a little defensive and uncertain about who you can trust with sensitive information about your son or daughter, be encouraged that you don't have to shout about your child's differences from the rooftops when you get to school. Your child doesn't have to wear a label on their chest that announces their challenges to the world, and if you ask them to keep information about your child and family confidential, most principals and deputy principals will respect your request.

Just as your child will forge new relationships next year, so will you. If you value the quality of the relationships you will make with teachers and other school staff, you will need to share the responsibility for making and keeping good connections.

Are you up for the challenge?

CHAPTER 8

SIX WAYS TO GET CONNECTED AT YOUR CHILD'S NEW SCHOOL

I have a group of five friends that calls itself 'The Inner Circle'. We met when our children were in Kindergarten, when one highly hospitable mum decided it would be nice to have a get together at her house. In the early days, a big crowd of mums would gather on the last Friday night of each term, and it quickly became apparent to me who the cool chicks in the room were. Five funny, smart, but all very different women seemed to naturally gravitate towards one another on the sofa in the middle of the room, and over time these five cool, interesting ladies became my friends.

Our original hostess, Holly, probably couldn't have imagined that the six of us would still be getting together at her house on the last day of term when our kids aren't even at school anymore, but such is the power of friendships forged at the school gate.

The Inner Circle has seen its members through thick and thin. Serious illness, divorces, kids acting crazy … you name it, we've laughed, cried and nibbled our way through kilos of cheese and bickies as we've held one another up, celebrated one another's successes and generally had each other's backs.

And more than a decade on from the time we first met, we wouldn't have it any other way.

HOW TO DEVELOP STRONG RELATIONSHIPS WITHIN THE SCHOOL COMMUNITY

Starting school is a new beginning for you and your child, and who knows, over time you might be lucky enough to build amazing relationships like I have.

Most schools roll out the welcome mat when new students and their families arrive, but getting to know teachers and other parents will require some effort on your part too.

The best way to build understanding at school is to be an active member of the community. When you get involved, not only do you get the chance to meet teachers in new contexts, but you meet other parents too. And remember, children love to see their mums and dads at school. When you get involved, you're not only giving your child the message that you value their education, but you also show the rest of the school community you appreciate what they are working towards and you want to play your part.

To help you develop strong relationships within the school community, here's six ways for you to help and get connected at your child's new school.

Get connected tip 1: Be a classroom helper

Many teachers appreciate and rely on the support of parents during busy times in the classroom, and being a classroom helper is a great way to observe your child in the context of his or her peers.

At the start of the year, teachers usually let parents know what kind of assistance they are looking for. The activities you might be able to put your hand up for include helping with:

- reading groups
- maths groups
- art and craft sessions
- weekly sport
- making props or costumes for a class performance.

Don't worry about not knowing what to do when you volunteer for these kinds of in-class roles. The teacher will know exactly what he or she needs you to do and will be grateful for your help.

If I can give you one extra tip though, don't commit to a promise you can't keep! Teachers will program their day around the planned activities you have said you'd be part of. If you can't be there on a regular basis, don't volunteer. The last thing you need is to start your relationship with the teacher with a quickly gained reputation for unreliability.

Get connected tip 2: Join the P & C

Joining the P & C is one of the best ways to get a sense of how your child's new school runs. P & C meetings usually only take place once or twice a term, so if you are a working parent who can't get to school during the day, they are a perfect opportunity to show your interest and get involved in your child's school in a meaningful way.

When you attend P & C meetings, you'll get an opportunity to meet teachers, talk with parents whose children may have been a part of the school for longer than yours, and contribute your thoughts, ideas and skills. As a newbie, no-one is expecting you to put your hand up to be the president, so don't worry about diving in at the deep end. Just show up and be interested. These out-of-hours meetings are a great way to let people get to know you and, through you, your child.

Get connected tip 3: Do canteen duty

Twenty-first-century school canteens are changing, so if you last went to the 'tuckshop' in 1997, you'll probably notice a few differences since your last visit. In Australia, school canteens are regulated by food safety regulations, and some even operate as standalone businesses. A growing number of schools now have online ordering systems which have replaced old-fashioned paper bags with orders scribbled on them. Favourite recess snacks like Cheezels and chips may be off the healthy menu at your child's new school too.

If your child's school has a canteen that's run on parent power, it offers a terrific opportunity to get involved with other mums, dads, teachers and students. Sure, you'll probably end up making forty-seven Vegemite sandwiches and three cheese salads, but as you do you'll get the chance to chat with other parents and learn about the school.

Some schools employ a coordinator who is paid to look after running the canteen, stock and rosters, so don't worry if you don't know what you are doing. If you have a day a month that you can give, the school will be grateful and your child will be thrilled to see you on the other side of the counter at lunchtime.

Six ways to get connected at your child's new school

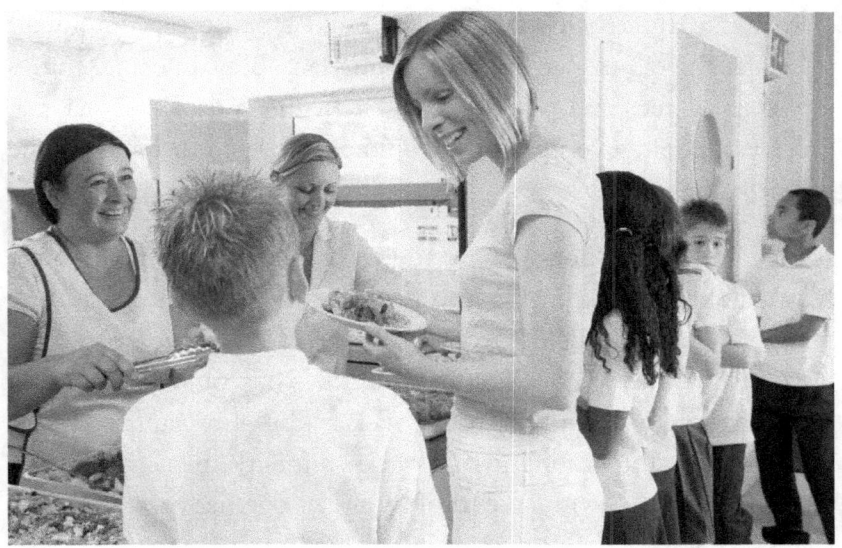

Get connected tip 4: Help in the library

Many parents don't realise that donating their time to the school library is an easy way to get involved at their child's school. With hundreds of books that need to be covered, repaired, stamped and catalogued every year, librarians need all the help they can get from interested parents who have an hour or two to spare. If time is hard to come by because you have work commitments or younger children to care for during the day, might you have time of an evening to roll out the contact and get your book-covering skills on? The school would appreciate your help.

Get connected tip 5: Volunteer to be Class Parent

I know. You've already got so much that you are responsible for, and the last thing you need is something else to organise, right? But, take it from me, taking on the role of Class Parent is a great way to get to know all the key players in your child's class next year.

The Class Parent helps the teacher build a sense of community by being the 'go-to person' for information about informal things like class picnics and group playdates. At the end of the year, the Class Parent often coordinates a common gift from the kids for the teacher too.

Being Class Parent doesn't have to take a lot of time, and if you're worried about not knowing anyone, this small role will give other parents a reason to talk to you and get to know you. If you don't want to take the whole thing on yourself, you could volunteer to share the role with another mum or dad who also wants to get to know people. You never know – your own Inner Circle could begin, just like mine did, with an end-of-term get together organised by a Class Parent.

Get connected tip 6: Share your skills

Every school has a finite number of teachers and lots of kids who have different interests and abilities. That's why teachers are always grateful when parents offer to share the load when it comes to organising activities that enhance the curriculum or give kids a chance to enjoy a new hobby. You might be a handy netballer, have a special interest in painting, or just be an excellent list maker and delegator. All of these skills could be used at school next year, and are another great way to meet people and indirectly build understanding for your child.

OTHER THINGS YOU CAN DO

Not sure if you have any skills that might be of value? Take a look at these other ideas and see if any of them resonate with you.

Six ways to get connected at your child's new school

If you're interested in sport or other physical activity, you could:

- run an after-school coaching clinic
- team up with one of the teachers to coach or manage a team
- volunteer to be a helper at weekly PE sessions.

If you have a special creative interest, you could:

- offer to help with the costumes for an assembly or concert performance
- assist the teacher who runs the school dance group or band
- give some time to the classroom teacher to help during art classes.

If you have administrative or IT skills, you could:

- work with the teacher to create a class newsletter or Facebook group
- help out in the classroom when the children are doing computer lessons
- offer to be a 'go to' person if the teacher needs emergency IT help
- lend a hand during big school events where IT and PA systems are used.

If you love to work in the garden, you could:

- lend a hand during working bees
- offer to help look after the school veggie patch
- liaise with the teacher to build a small class garden or sow seeds in pots so the children can watch them grow
- volunteer to help the teacher who coordinates the school's environment club.

If you are a keen cook, you could:

- contribute to cake stalls, school fetes or a monthly charity drive
- consult with the principal to see if there is a way you can make an occasional meal for a family in the school community who might be struggling (this happens more often than you might think)
- coordinate with other parents to cater for a monthly morning tea for the school staff.

If you have extended periods of time available, you could:

- volunteer to be an excursion helper
- be an extra adult supervisor for a school camp.

Remember, even if you don't think you have any specific skills, if you have two hands and are willing to help you will always be welcome at your child's school. There are many incidental ways in which you can get involved at school, and every time you do, you'll get chances to meet and talk with teachers and parents.

So next year, don't be shy! If volunteers are sought to help out at open day, or if tired teachers simply need someone to help them put chairs and tables away after a P & C meeting, lend a hand. You might be surprised at how those small moments add up over time, and how you and your child will benefit from getting to know the teachers and parents of your child's school in settings that go beyond the boundaries of the classroom.

THERE'S NO HURRY

As the first day of school gets closer and you start to speculate about what other parents will think of you, try to remember that they are probably feeling the same way you are.

Every family who has a child starting school for the first time wonders whether they will fit in. The fact that you have a child with unique needs doesn't make you any different to the other mums and dads who will be standing around, perhaps a little awkwardly, when the children are led off to class on those first few days of school.

Everyone will be looking to someone else to make the first move to introduce themselves with a friendly smile. Could that person be you?

The bottom line is that you're going to meet lots of other parents and carers during your child's school journey. Most of them will seem very nice and you'll have many a cordial chat about lost lunchboxes and upcoming excursions. There may be a clique or two, and that's okay. Groups of veteran school mums who already know each other through their older children are likely to gather together, so don't take it personally if you're not included in their conversations.

Eventually, though, if you're brave and just being yourself, faces will become familiar. Conversations will start more naturally, a cup of coffee might be shared, and before you know it, you've made your first 'school parent' friend.

Just as it takes children time to adjust to the social dynamic of a peer group, it also takes time for parents to feel confident and comfortable at their child's school. So hang in there and be prepared to keep saying hello to people you don't know.

Who knows? Over time, a fledgling friendship just may be formed.

You're likely to be seeing these people for years to come, so there's no rush. The kindred spirit you're searching for may also be looking for you. In the long run, the time it takes to find one another will have been worth the wait.

PART III

FITTING IN AND MAKING FRIENDS

If you're lying awake at night hoping and praying that you and your child will be part of a welcoming, understanding community next year, you are not alone.

We all want our kids to feel like they belong when they start school. We want them to feel accepted by their peers and we want them to find a friend so that they don't have to face the demands of the classroom and playground on their own.

And if we are really honest with ourselves, the hopes and dreams we have for our child are ones that we quietly have for ourselves too. Being the parent of a sensitive child with unique needs can be hard sometimes, and it's normal to wonder if you will find a kindred spirit at the school gate who will make the journey you are about to embark on a little easier.

A crystal ball would be handy in moments like this, wouldn't it?

So let's talk about the hopes and dreams we all have for our kids, and how to make them happen.

CHAPTER 9

FINDING BELONGING AND ACCEPTANCE

'When we got here we found out that because Hannah had turned five the previous year, she had to start school at the end of January. We'd left the UK after Christmas hoping that we could ease our way in to life in Australia, but it turned out to be exactly the opposite. My husband had his work, but I was in a new place with three children aged under six. Hannah had missed all the school orientation days and was fretting for her friends and family at home. I didn't know a soul here and neither did she. I tried to put on a brave face on her first day at school, but deep inside I felt completely lost, and I think she did too.'

Bronwen, Hannah's mum

Bronwen and her family had only been in Australia for about three weeks when her daughter Hannah started school. Bronwen's British husband had been promoted to a new role in Sydney, and while the opportunity to live and work in our sunburnt country was exciting, she also found it overwhelming. She was lonely, under pressure, and – because she didn't know anybody at Hannah's new school – worried that the isolation she felt would be permanent.

If you, like Bronwen, are concerned about the social side of your child's schooling next year, you're not alone. I have spoken with thousands of parents over the years, and I don't think I've ever met a mum or a dad who hasn't placed their child's happiness at the top of their going-to-school wish list.

To be truly happy at school, children have to feel like they belong there.

And, just quietly, isn't a sense of belonging what we want for ourselves too?

As the parents of a sensitive child, it's quite possible that, just as you are looking for a community that will value your child, you're also searching for your own 'tribe'. A group like my 'Inner Circle', perhaps, where you'll find common ground, support and the opportunity to enjoy a laugh or two.

The question is, how can you make this happen?

Well, the truth is that there are some things you can do, and there are some things you can't do when it comes to helping your child with unique needs feel like he or she belongs at school.

So let's stop and think about that for a moment.

WHAT WERE YOUR SCHOOL YEARS LIKE?

You might be one of the many fortunate adults who can look back fondly on their school years as a happy time filled with friends and youthful adventures. You may even be lucky enough, as some people are, to be blessed with life-long friendships that started in the playground and continue to this day.

It's normal and natural to want your child to experience the same sense of connection, trust and understanding you have enjoyed. It's also normal to worry if your child with unique needs seems to find it harder to connect with other kids than you did.

On the other hand, if your memories of school are not positive, you might know exactly what feeling excluded and isolated is like. If you struggled to find likeminded peers when you were at school, it's perfectly reasonable to hope that your child's experience of school will be better than yours was.

FINDING BELONGING

Have you ever worked in an environment where you felt like you just didn't fit in? Or gone to a social function where the rest of the guests ignored you?

It's not a nice feeling, is it?

As adults, we've all experienced uncomfortable moments in our lives, but because we're grown-ups, we can usually see the big picture. We might recognise that the boss is a bully and find a way to work around him, or see that the host is run off her feet after a catering disaster and therefore we don't take her failure to introduce us to other guests to heart. Because we have the experience, perspective and power to make decisions about what we will do and say in those kinds of awkward social situations, we are able to navigate our way through them. We don't always enjoy it, but we manage it.

When little children feel like they don't fit in, it's a lot harder for them to cope.

Five year olds rarely have the social and emotional maturity to understand why other children exclude them. Because they are so young, their self-awareness isn't well developed. They don't recognise how their own words and actions impact others, and if their problem-solving skills aren't great, little issues can quickly become big problems that affect their confidence and wellbeing.

Belonging helps kids feel happy and relaxed at school

According to *KidsMatter,* an initiative of the Australian Government that supports children's wellbeing and mental health, children who feel as though they belong at school 'are happier, more relaxed and have fewer behavioural problems than other students'.[8]

This is what we all want for our kids, right?

---

[8] KidsMatter. Belonging at school makes a difference, © Commonwealth of Australia 2008.

Feeling a sense of belonging next year will not only be important for your child's social and emotional wellbeing, it will also give your son or daughter the best chance of learning and meeting their potential, whatever that might be.

Welcome mats and red carpets

As you and your child with unique needs start school next year, it's quite possible that the school will roll out the red carpet to welcome you both.

Orientations days, morning teas, information evenings and an open invitation to attend the first P & C meeting of the year may be just some of the early opportunities you might have to meet and greet teachers and parents. If the school has a peer support program, an older student might take your little one under their wing in the playground, and teachers could stagger starts to recess and lunchtime so that your son or daughter is gradually introduced to the hustle and bustle of the school yard.

It's quite possible that the first few weeks of school will feel fabulous, and you might wonder why you ever worried about your child not fitting in. This flurry of social activity is often typical at the start of the year. You and your child will probably enjoy the special efforts that are made to help you settle in, and you might even be lulled into the expectation that this is what life at school will be like forever.

The reality is, though, that once initial overtures of welcome are made by the school and the people who are part of it, it will be left to you and your child to respond. Within a few weeks, the personal invitations you've received will be replaced by general notifications in the school newsletter. Year Six buddies will return to playmates of their own age, and the early starts to recess and lunchtime which gave your child the chance to explore the playground in the absence of bigger kids will end.

Suddenly, being at your child's new school might not seem very comfortable, but if you hang in there, things will get easier.

It takes time

When we truly belong to a community, we feel familiar and comfortable there. It's not something that happens overnight, and there will be many other families who are newcomers just like you.

It's probably going to take you and your sensitive child some time to settle in, so go with the flow and get involved with as many things as you can. Remember, the more people you meet, the more opportunities you will have to meet likeminded families that have things in common with yours.

FINDING ACCEPTANCE

> 'All of a sudden, Riley just couldn't bear to be apart from me. Drop offs at preschool were a nightmare because he was frightened that I was going to leave him and not come back like Lee and his Nana did. By the time he started school, I knew that his clinginess was a problem, but it was hard to tell people why he was so upset. I was grieving too, and it was hard to talk about such personal things with strangers.'
>
> *Suzanne, Riley's mum*

Suzanne's son, Riley, started school after a particularly rocky time in his family. In the year before Kindergarten began, his much-loved grandmother passed away suddenly. Several months later, Suzanne's relationship with her partner, Lee, broke down. Lee moved interstate, and Riley, who had previously been quite a confident child, began to suffer from extreme separation anxiety.

You might be able to relate to this because, at times, the things that make our children unique are intensely personal.

Just like Suzanne, you might be wondering about what other people are going to think if they find out what lies beneath the surface of your child's challenges. If past experiences at preschool, daycare and even within your own family have been filled with judgement and misunderstanding, it's natural to feel reluctant about baring your soul to people you've only just met. Your protective instincts for your child and your family will of course kick in as you try to navigate a new environment where everything and everyone is unfamiliar.

If you're looking for acceptance, but are afraid you won't find it when your child starts school next year, you are not alone.

The importance of acceptance

As human beings, we all crave acceptance. We fear rejection too because, as a species, we are social animals.

Our ancient ancestors lived in a world where acceptance had life or death consequences. Survival often depended on the group's acceptance and help, and rejection could mean a death sentence if a person or family was excluded.

In Australia today, acceptance may not have the same life or death consequences that our ancestors experienced, yet with mental health being such a widespread challenge for children and adults in our country today, feeling accepted is just as important now as it has always been.

Feeling accepted is important for you.

It's important for me.

It's important for our children. And the way they feel when they are at school has an impact on their social, emotional and academic wellbeing.

As parents of sensitive children with unique needs, it's normal and natural to worry about whether our kids will be accepted when they start school. Sitting on the sidelines while a child struggles is not easy, and sometimes the insensitive things that other people say can make the hurt even harder to bear.

But have hope – finding the acceptance you are searching for may not be as hard as it seems.

Finding acceptance at school

In accepting your child's enrolment, your child's new school has sent you a message that it wants your child, and your family, to be part of its community. While there might be challenges ahead, a mutual willingness to give it a go is a positive place to start in any relationship, and it's worth remembering when late-night worries about fitting in start to get you down.

The staff you will be entrusting your child to are professional educators who are used to working closely with parents and carers. Many schools have specialist teachers whose role it is to support children with unique needs. Other staff might have significant professional or personal experience in the very thing that your child needs to succeed at school, and so putting the pieces of the puzzle together with these people will be an important part of gaining teacher acceptance and understanding.

Support, when sought the right way and from the right people, is never far away when children are at school. Within the school you will find senior staff such as the principal, assistant principal and school counsellor upon whom you can call, and outside the school you may find that the network, diocese or education system to which your child's school belongs also has support services you can utilise.

Meeting half way

Sometimes it takes time to win the acceptance of people who don't know you.

When your child starts school next year, you may be fortunate enough to meet, or be introduced to, other parents who share the challenges you and your child face and with whom you feel an instant connection. You could be welcomed with open arms into a community that prides itself on a culture of inclusion, and where acceptance and support are part of the school's ethos. Equally, it's also possible that your child's needs are not commonly understood and that building the foundations for acceptance could take a while.

Remember, the responsibility for creating an environment of acceptance and understanding runs both ways. People will only accept and understand you if they have the chance to get to know you, so you will need to be willing to meet other families half way and be as interested in them as you hope they will be in you.

Helping your child to develop the skills he or she needs to be accepted by the other kids will also be your responsibility.

Five year olds often don't see difference, and your child's new classmates might surprise you with their willingness to include your child with unique needs. However, if your little boy or girl needs extra help to learn how to connect with other kids, schools can only do so much. Make sure you obtain expert advice from specialists who can help you bridge social or learning gaps, such as speech pathologists, occupational therapists, special educators and psychologists. Their advice and guidance could make a huge difference to the way in which your sensitive child interacts with others.

PROTECTING YOUR PRIVACY

You are completely entitled to keep information about your child's unique needs private. Schools and teachers are well aware that maintaining your child's confidentiality is one of their most important professional obligations, and unless staff have your specific permission, they should not share information about your child with any unauthorised person.

Having said that, some families prefer to take a proactive approach to sharing information about their child's unique needs with classmates and their families. For example, the parents of children who have diagnosed disabilities, hearing problems, sight impairments or mobility issues sometimes choose to work with teachers, special educators and other professionals to build specific social and educational inclusion opportunities for their children. You might decide that disclosing details of your child's challenges in a positive and sensitive way is preferable to a 'wait and see' approach, and if this is the case, there are a few things that you can do to help this process to happen.

Government or systemic schools often have access to the support of specialist staff who consult to schools in the region to resource students with unique needs, their families and teachers. If your child will be attending one of these kinds of schools next year, these experienced teachers may have wisdom to share about how to effectively communicate your child's needs to the rest of the community.

Similarly, if your child has a specific disability that you would like their teachers and peers to understand better, your child's new school may also be open to utilising external organisations that specialise in delivering professional development programs for teachers and peer education activities for groups of students. Autism Spectrum Australia (Aspect) and Down Syndrome Australia are just two of the many services that support school-aged children in this way, so if you are keen to explore this option, some time spent researching what is on offer might be helpful before school begins so that you can talk with teachers when the time is right.

HAVE REALISTIC EXPECTATIONS

Belonging and acceptance are important, and when you find them among teachers, parents and other children this is something you will come to treasure.

Be patient, hang in there, and for your child's sake, have the courage to occasionally step out of your comfort zone. If you get involved in school life, keep showing up, and are open to meeting new people, you and your child will gradually become known for the people you are, not the challenges that your child has.

CHAPTER 10

FINDING FRIENDSHIP

'To me, it didn't matter if Gretel wasn't at the top of the class. I didn't care if she wasn't the best at maths or the fastest reader, but the thing that I really worried about was whether she would be able to make a friend.'

Sani, Gretel's mum

Sani discovered that her daughter, Gretel, had an expressive and receptive language delay when Gretel was about three. Although Gretel attended weekly speech therapy sessions and went to pre-school three days a week, it was always easier for her to interact with adults – who made allowances for her difficulties – than children, whose unpredictable games and conversations she struggled to understand. As Sani prepared Gretel to start school, she knew that her daughter's unique needs would be catered for in the classroom, but she was worried about how she would cope in the playground.

If your child's preschool years have been more challenging than you expected, you might be hoping that going to school will give your child the social success that has eluded them until now. Being able to make and keep friends is one of the most important skills children develop in their early years. While some kids find it easy to be social because they are naturally gregarious, or come from big families where negotiating and compromising is part of life, others struggle to find likeminded mates and a 'tribe' to which they can belong.

If you're worried your child is going to fall into the latter category when school starts next year, you are not alone.

THE ABILITY TO MAKE FRIENDS IS A LEARNED SKILL

As children grow and develop, so too do their social skills. It's a step-by-step process that requires children to not only use their speech and language skills, but also to regulate emotions such as excitement, anxiety and frustration.

Without wanting to dive too deeply into psychology and the vast amount of research that's been done on the topic of children's social skills, I thought it might be helpful to share some ideas about friendship that come from Professor Robert L. Selman, a respected psychologist at Harvard University.[9]

Professor Selman's many published works explain that, as children grow and develop, their perspectives on friendships change. Instead of using the complicated language of psychological therapy, I've created a basic summary of some of his ideas below.

---

[9] Selman, RL (1981). 'The Child as Friendship Philosopher'. In SR Asher and JM Gottman (Eds.), *The Development of Children's Friendships*, Cambridge: Cambridge University Press (pp. 242–72).

Where do you think your child's social skills are at right now?

'Momentary' mates

Professor Selman says that many children aged between three and six view friends as momentary playmates who think in the same way they do. They don't understand, or frankly care, about the perspectives of other people, and their main priority in play is simply having fun together. If this is where your child is at right now, they might happily join forces with new kids each time you go to the park, but not yet have formed any strong attachments to the children they see every day at preschool. The concept of having a 'best friend' is not yet on their radar, and this is quite age-appropriate, so don't panic about your child's social skills yet.

'I like you when you do it my way' friends

According to Professor Selman, children aged five to nine often fall into this zone. Kids at this level of social development understand that friendship is a two-way thing, but they much prefer it when things go their way than someone else's. These children think about friendship in a very matter-of-fact way. To them, a friend is someone who makes friendly gestures towards them, like offering to share a lunchbox treat or saving a seat on the bus, but they don't really think about what they themselves contribute to the relationship. If your child is at this level of development, he or she may care a lot about friendship and be starting to understand the importance of fitting in. They may even put up with a not-so-nice friend, just so they can have someone to hang around with.

'Fair weather' friends

Children who have developed this approach to friendship are usually aged seven to twelve. While your child might not be at this

point now, the older children in their class may start to think this way as the first year of school progresses, so it's helpful to know what lies ahead on the social skills horizon. Children who are at this stage of development get the idea that friendship is a reciprocal thing, but it's still hard for them to think about their friend's needs and their own at the same time. They like to be friends when the going is good, but they're less enthusiastic about working through problems, and this can particularly happen with girls, whose friendships at this age can be fickle to say the least. These kids understand the concept of taking turns and other playground conventions, but they still might miss cues that suggest other kids are manipulating or taking advantage of them.

This might be a little way down the track for your school starter, but it's worth knowing that they might need a bit of resilience to cope with the jealousy, judgements and a desire to fit in that are common aspects of friendships for children going through this social skills phase. Small friendship groups based around similar interests, sometimes known as 'secret clubs', may not be part of your child's playground experience next year, but by the end of Year One, elaborate rules and lots of discussion about who is or isn't included as a member might begin.

* * *

When you read all of this, you'd be forgiven for thinking that some of the adults you know have little chance of ever developing these skills, let alone hoping that your five year old will master them in the next twelve months! I don't include this information to freak you out, but rather to give you a bit of a 'heads up' on what the social landscape is going to look like when your child is established at school.

Making and keeping friends is a challenge for all children, not just those with unique needs. However, if you have an idea of where your child is at now, it will help you as you support your child's social skills in the years ahead.

FRIENDSHIP SKILLS START AT HOME

When my son was little, I spent hours playing 'shops' with him in our backyard cubby house. When his grandparents came over, they played shops too, and when his cousins visited, guess what? The store was open for business.

The idea of this game was to give my preschooler a repertoire of words and phrases he could use when he met new children at our local park. I lost count of the number of times I sold him an imaginary banana or he took my order for a packet of biscuits, but every moment of backyard bargaining was worth it when I took him to the park and watched him happily engage in pretend play with kids he'd never met before.

In the next few months before school begins, you might find yourself doing the same kinds of things with your child because children learn through play and that starts at home.

If you expect that your child will be able to pull social skills out of their pocket when they are in a new and stressful environment such as a crowded park or playground, you are likely to be disappointed. Very few children are able to master the demands of play unless they have had plenty of practice in the safety and comfort of their home first.

If making and keeping friends is a challenge for your child, do yourself and your child a favour: don't expect that your child's social skills will just 'kick in'. Start early, introduce new social skills at home, get advice, and enlist help if you have to.

Your child's early educators will probably be able to give you great insights about your child's social interactions with other children. Find out what your child is good at and where your child could do with some help, and use this information to support the play skills you teach at home.

Of course, you don't have to do it all yourself. If an older sibling, cousin, aunt, uncle or grandparent is willing to join your child for some play-based learning, your child will get valuable practice playing with people whose play routines are not as predictable for them as yours. All of this will stand your child in good stead as the time for school rolls around.

PRESCHOOL IS A GOOD START, BUT ...

As you and I know, making a friend involves being a friend.

If your child attends preschool or daycare, that's great, but to really be ready for the demands of 'big school', opportunities to meet other children in less predictable environments are the way to go.

Parks, beaches, story time at the local library and playdates with friends' children are just some of the ways in which you can start stretching your child's social-skill muscles in the coming months, but before you embark on your mission to find a friend for your child, may I offer a word of caution?

It doesn't matter if you are five or fifty-five. Getting good at something takes time and repetition.

Think about the last time you learned something new.

Did you 'get it' straight away? Or did you have to try, try and try again before you managed to master the skill you were aiming to acquire?

As you focus on supporting your child's social skills in the next few months, remember that these things don't magically appear just because we want them to. It might take 30 visits to a park before your child is able to remember all the steps involved in meeting and greeting a child they've never met before. It's quite possible that, in the midst of excitement, social anxiety and the desire to be the boss of the game, your five year old will forget almost everything you have spent hours teaching. But if a little bit of progress is made each time, your efforts will be rewarded.

'WHO DID YOU PLAY WITH TODAY?'

Are you guilty of interrogating your child about their social life at the end of each preschool day? We all want our children to have friends, and when our sons and daughters can tell us the names of their playmates, it's natural to breathe a sigh of relief, safe in the knowledge that they haven't been wandering around the playground on their own.

But what happens when your child routinely tells you that they didn't play with anyone? Do you worry your child is being left out of games, or doesn't know how to join in?

Some children do struggle to connect in the playground, but experienced teachers will tell you there's often another reason for kids' vague answers to their parents' questions. You see, young children are often so busy socialising that the name of their playmate is quite irrelevant to them.

Your five year old is probably focused on having fun when they play. Committing every moment to memory so that they can give you a blow-by-blow description of what they did, who they did it with and how long they did it for is not really their priority.

When you ask 'Who did you play with today?' four hours after the game ended, your child may answer with 'no-one' simply because they honestly can't remember.

It can be frustrating, and even worrying when this happens frequently, but here's a simple way to ask the same question in a slightly different way. Instead of using a direct question like 'Who did you play with today?', ask your child 'Did you play with *someone* today?'

The answer is likely to be easier for them to give, and in return, you'll get a much better idea of how your child's friendship skills are faring.

TIPS FOR POSITIVE PLAYDATES

It's all very well for me to advise you to get your child out and about in order to practise their social skills, but it would be remiss of me to not mention some ways to make these playdates as positive as possible.

You know your child best, so make sure you use your knowledge to its full advantage when introducing your son or daughter to new places and faces.

If you have a reserved, anxious child, you might need to take things slowly with social activities that are short and sweet. You may need to start off with a park or playground that doesn't become crowded with kids, so that your preschooler is not overwhelmed.

If you have a rambunctious, active and slightly over-the-top youngster, choosing the right place and time to meet new people will also be important. The last thing you need is an over-tired, over-stimulated five year old whose playground excitement turns into a meltdown at the slightest provocation, so before you head out the door, make sure your child is well rested and well fed.

> **SCHOOL READY TOOLKIT**
>
> If you want to get creative with the social opportunities you offer your child before school begins, I've added some of my favourite ideas for making and keeping friends to the *School Ready Toolkit* that accompanies this book. Go to www.kids-first.com.au or www.sonjawalker.com.au and use the unique code SchoolReady to download your free copy.

WHAT'S HARRY POTTER GOT TO DO WITH IT?

I frequently present seminars for parents, and when the subject of making and keeping friends pops up, as it often does, I usually talk about Harry Potter. You see, Harry didn't need a big gang of friends to feel safe, cared for and valued. As long as Ron and Hermione had his back, he was okay.

The same may be true for your little boy or girl next year. The large group of friends you are hoping for might not eventuate, but if your child is able to make one or two connections, that's a goal worth aiming for.

Making and keeping friends is complicated for little kids, and it's not uncommon for young children to struggle in the unstructured environment of a school playground where there are no adults to keep everything in order. In the coming months, setting social rules and helping your sensitive child learn to negotiate them will be some of the most important preparation you do before school begins.

School playgrounds can be fun places, but they can be full of impenetrable groups too. Try not to worry about whether your child will be part of the group. All your child will need is the skills to find their own Ron or Hermione.

In the beginning, having just one friend will do.

PART IV

CLOSING THE GAP

Every single one of the children who will start school in Australia next year is unique, and therefore it would be fair to say that they all have unique needs.

Most will be excited about starting 'big school', and in preschools around the country they will be practising their pencil grip and scissor skills, as well as learning about shapes, colours and sounds. Pretty soon, their parents will be wondering about the best time to buy uniforms and school shoes, and backpacks, pencil cases and library bags will all be chosen with care.

But for sensitive children like yours and mine, the next few months might be spent jumping slightly higher hurdles because parents like you and I will be trying to help our kids get up to speed with skills that their peers might take for granted.

Our children demonstrate behaviours that the rest of their peers don't display, well at least not in public anyway. The things other kids find easy are still a challenge for our sons and daughters, and we're worried that the difference is going to be noticeable next year. So, for us, the next few months will be spent trying to 'close the gaps' so that our children's challenges have as little impact as possible when they start school.

If your child is struggling with separation anxiety, you're probably going to be focusing on building courage. If your child finds it hard to follow toileting routines, developing independence could be your goal. If fussy eating means your child has a limited diet, you'll be looking for solutions at lunchtime, and if emotional meltdowns are a daily occurrence at your house, you'll be working on regulation and resilience.

It's easy to look around at school information nights and think you are the only parent in the crowd who is worrying about more than early literacy and lunchboxes.

But take heart.

There are lots of mums and dads who are trying to close gaps with their children before school begins. Whether it's obvious or not, you're not the only one whose child's personality is a little 'left of centre' and skills are somewhere 'outside the square'.

You might not realise it yet, but you're definitely not alone.

CHAPTER 11

DON'T LEAVE ME!

'I was so embarrassed. Emily just cried hysterically and her whole body shook with fear. Every time I tried to let go of her hand she'd hide under my legs, and eventually she just lay on the ground and screamed. I'd spent weeks talking to Emily about big school and the teachers were very understanding, but on that day I realised that we still had a long way to go.'

Belinda, Emily's mum

Belinda's daughter, Emily, struggled with separation anxiety as a preschooler. When Belinda took Emily to her first primary school orientation day, Emily had a meltdown of volcanic proportions when teachers tried to take her into the classroom with the other children.

Sound familiar?

If your child, like Emily, has an impressive range of avoidance behaviours which have been making it hard to say goodbye for a while, it's perfectly understandable that you are worried about how your son or daughter will cope when school starts next year.

Although you probably already know that separation anxiety is typical in very young children and have possibly read every book and article you could about the subject, it doesn't make it any easier in the heat of the moment. When the other kids race into the pre-school classroom with barely a 'Bye Mum' and you are left struggling with a clingy, soggy limpet who refuses to let you out of their grasp, it's easy to think that you are the only parent in the group who has to go through this kind of emotional ordeal every day.

Take heart, because you're not.

SEPARATION ANXIETY IS MORE COMMON THAN YOU THINK

According to Professor Ron Rapee, from Macquarie University's Department of Psychology and Centre for Emotional Health in Sydney, about 5 per cent of Australian children meet the criteria for an anxiety disorder at some stage during their lifetime.[10] Your child might be one of the many who finds it hard to put their feelings of fear into words, and as your child starts school next year it's quite likely there is a small fleet of families who are sailing in a boat that's similar to yours.

Despite your efforts to get your child used to leaving you, meltdowns at preschool might be just one of the challenges you routinely face with your sensitive, anxious child who refuses point

---

10   Rapee RM. 'Anxiety Disorders in Children and Adolescents: Nature, development, treatment and prevention'. In JM Rey (Ed.), *IACAPAP e-Textbook of Child and Adolescent Mental Health*, Geneva: International Association for Child and Adolescent Psychiatry and Allied Professions 2012.

blank to face any situation that involves being away from you. Your strong-willed five year old may be deeply attached to you and worried that something might happen to you if you are apart. Visits to relatives and friends might be tricky, and staying at home in the company of a babysitter absolutely impossible.

It's hard, but there is some light at the end of the tunnel.

Most teachers have plenty of experience helping anxious new students overcome their reluctance to go to school, and will be willing to work with you to help your child settle in. If you already know that this need is one your child is likely to have next year, the earlier you get started, the better. Supporting an anxious child takes lots of time, patience and teamwork, but trust me, the long-term results of building your child's resilience will be worth it.

MUMS AND DADS HOLD THE KEY

It's understandable that you might be nervous about sending your child into an unfamiliar environment for the first time next year.

Parents play a vital part in modelling confident behaviours to their children, so managing your own emotions will be one of the most important ways in which you can help your child manage theirs as school begins.

Anxious children are often very 'tuned in' to their parents. You might have already noticed that your child takes their emotional cues from you, and that the way in which you respond to situations is a bit of a barometer for your child's behaviour.

Research has also shown that anxiety runs in families.[11] If you, or another family member, are a sensitive person who is prone to feelings of worry, it's quite possible your child has inherited this trait, along with the blue eyes or brown hair that other members of your clan have in common.

Sometimes, children's separation anxiety can be closely linked to the anxiety felt by their parent. Of course, this is not deliberate, but over-protective mums and dads who tend to 'cotton wool' their kids can contribute to the challenges their children face.

To make a successful start to school, your child will need an age-appropriate sense of self that is separate from you. If you find yourself frequently giving in to your child's demands, constantly reassuring your child or letting your child sleep with you because it makes it easier for you to manage stressful situations, it might be worth thinking about how your responses are affecting your child's ability to build resilience.

In the next few months you have a great opportunity to develop that skill before school starts.

---

11 Rapee, RM (2012). 'Family Factors in the Development and Management of Anxiety Disorders', *Clinical Child and Family Psychology Review*, Vol. 15, Issue 1, pp. 69–80.

SEPARATION ANXIETY IS DIFFICULT TO OVERCOME

If your child struggles with separation anxiety, it's quite possible he or she worries that any, or all, of the following things could happen to you while you are apart:

- you will forget about them
- you won't return and they will be left behind
- something bad will happen to you.

While you and I know these things are unlikely to occur, it's difficult for an anxious five year old to understand these very abstract concepts. These fears will often raise their ugly heads many times before your child learns to trust that they will be okay without you.

Ask any adult who has a phobia about snakes or spiders and they'll tell you it's not easy for an anxious person to overcome something they are frightened of. While their fears might not be sensible or rational to others, they are very real to the person involved. If your child struggles with separation anxiety, the same may be true. Little kids don't have the advanced cognitive skills needed to troubleshoot unhelpful thoughts, and that's where you and other caring grown-ups come in.

It's going to take time and a gentle step-by-step approach to overcome kicking, screaming 'don't leave me' terror. If you leave it too late to start practising, the pressure of being apart will weigh heavily on you and your child in January next year. By starting now, you will give your child hundreds of opportunities to learn they don't need you to be their personal security blanket. Their world will open up to new people, new friends and new possibilities, and that's the whole point of going to school, right?

'SEE YOU LATER' STRATEGIES

Over the next few months it's really important to give your sensitive child positive experiences of separating from you and then reuniting with you. These are the things that will help your son or daughter to develop the confidence and the resilience to be able to say goodbye at the start of their first school day.

Avoiding separations because your child becomes upset just makes it harder in the long run, so right now is the time to start developing 'see you later' routines that will help your child to build trust and confidence. The internet is full of practical ideas and reputable sites like KidsMatter (www.kidsmatter.edu.au) and the Raising Children Network (www.raisingchildren.net.au), and these are just two of the free sources you can look to for ideas that could help your family.

> **SCHOOL READY TOOLKIT**
>
> My *Strategies for Managing Separation Anxiety* are also included in the School Ready Toolkit that accompanies this book. Go to www.kids-first.com.au or www.sonjawalker.com.au and use the unique code SchoolReady to download your free copy.

SIX TOP TIPS TO LEARN TO SAY GOODBYE

There are lots of things you can do to support your child's resilience, but if I had to give you my six top tips for helping your child learn to say goodbye without tears, they would be:

1. Remember why you chose the school in the first place.
2. Keep a relaxed and happy look on your face.

3   Tell your child when you're leaving and when you'll be coming back.

4   Have a predictable morning routine.

5   Have a 'see you later spot'.

6   Seek expert help if you need it.

Let's have a look at each of these.

Top tip 1: Remember why you chose the school in the first place

Do you remember the first day you visited the school your child will attend next year? You were no doubt impressed by the professionalism shown by the teachers and the rest of the school's staff. Impressed enough, I would suggest, to feel that you could trust these knowledgeable and highly trained people to teach, care for and inspire your son or daughter as they start school. If your sensitive child struggles to be apart from you, you may need to draw on that trust if anxiety kicks in next year. Your little one might be upset, and there's every chance you could be too, but the teachers you will be handing your child to are likely to be very experienced educators who have supported many a school starter. Teachers often say that a child who seems very distressed when their parents are present often settles quite quickly when mummy and daddy have left.

If separation anxiety is a challenge for your child, remember that teachers are on your side, and they want the very best for your child. Trust them when they tell you they will look after your little one, and believe them when they tell you they will call you if they need to.

Top tip 2: Keep a relaxed and happy look on your face

If you look sad or worried, your child is likely to think they're not safe in their environment and this will make it harder for them to separate from you. Regardless of whether you are farewelling your child as you leave them at preschool or their grandparents' house, soft words and a calm expression on your face are what's needed as you gently, but firmly, say goodbye. If your child's distress upsets you, try not to let it show. If you need to shed a tear in the car, by all means have a packet of tissues handy, but if your child sees you cry, his or her distress will amplify, and that's not the aim of the game.

Top tip 3: Tell your child when you're leaving and when you'll be coming back

Some parents try to sneak away in the hope that their anxious child will become engrossed in play and won't notice they are gone. Let's get real here. This rarely happens, and kids do notice. If you try this tactic and your child realises you have left without saying goodbye, it can deepen their fear of being left behind. Mummies and daddies who break their children's trust make it harder for their children to let them go next time. Don't be that parent. Be honest with your child, and make sure you keep your word. Tell your child when you are leaving and come back when you say will, so that your child can have confidence in what you say and do.

Top tip 4: Have a predictable morning routine

Children need the security of routines to help them feel safe about new experiences. So as you're going to preschool, Kindy and long daycare in the coming months, have a predictable morning routine you follow every day. Sometimes it's easier said than done when you are trying to get little people out the door on time, but the more organised you are at home, the better your chance of having a child whose emotions are not at tipping point the moment they get into the car.

Small 'night-before' hacks like preparing clothing and lunches for the following day can make a huge difference to 7.00 am stress levels for everyone, and especially your child with unique needs. At preschool, try to say goodbye in the same way every day. Hand your child over to the same staff member at the same time in the same way if you can. The calmer you are, the calmer your child will be, and at drop-off time this will make life easier for everyone.

Top tip 5: Have a 'see you later spot'

A specific place in which you say goodbye to your child can be a helpful thing to build into your farewell routine. The 'see you later' spot is like an imaginary line which you don't cross over, no matter how hard your son begs or how loudly your daughter cries.

Staff from your child's early childhood centre might be able to help you choose a location that works so your child's 'see you later spot' doesn't affect other families as they come and go. If you can get your son or daughter comfortable with this concept this year, your child will be better able to use it again in other situations, such as visits to grandparents or when school begins next year. The door of the classroom, a window through which they can wave goodbye, or a step near the entrance to the building are all good places to start. And as your child's resilience grows next year, the distance between your 'see you later' spot and the classroom can increase bit by bit.

Top tip 6: Seek expert help if you need it

If you find that you're out of your depth when it comes to helping your anxious child separate from you, it's worth seeking help from an expert in children's learning and development. Children

whose anxiety goes unaddressed when they are little can miss out on developing the resilience they need for learning and life.

You want your child to have the confidence to make friends, reach their academic potential and participate in the fun things that are part of going to school, like sleepovers, camps, excursions and other extracurricular activities, don't you? If your son's or daughter's anxiety is impacting on his or her ability to do what other children of the same age take for granted, you should take it seriously.

Often, someone who is 'outside the emotional bubble' of your family might be able to see things that you can't and suggest strategies you haven't thought of. The director of your child's early childhood education centre and experienced teachers may be able to help. Similarly, a psychologist who works with children and families can provide evidence-based advice and ideas so you and your child can find a way to move forward.

Trust me, the time and effort you take to get expert advice and support now will be worth it when your child starts school next year.

CHAPTER 12

NUMBER ONES AND NUMBER TWOS

'Lachie really struggles with toilets. When he was two and three, he resisted every effort I made to get him out of nappies. He'd just sit on the toilet, do nothing and wait until I put his nappy back on to do his thing. Eventually, when he was four, I got him out of nappies and he would wear a pull-up to preschool. The staff were fine with it, but the only problem was that he refused to use any toilet other than the one at home. It didn't matter how much gentle encouragement his teachers gave or how many rewards I offered, nothing worked to change his mind. Lachie would hang on all day and then be bursting to go by the time we got in the door. The same thing happened if we went shopping or even to visit his grandmother. He had quite a few accidents in the car, and I didn't know how he was going to manage on his own when he went to school.'

Gina, Lachlan's mum

To most people, Gina's son Lachlan looks like a typically developing five year old. With his big brown eyes, chatty personality and impressive knowledge of dinosaurs, few would know that Lachlan has an invisible difficulty that Gina worried about constantly as his time to start school approached.

Going to the toilet is not something that parents of four and five year olds talk about in public very often. Let's face it, most preschoolers master the art of number ones and number twos by the time they start preschool, and it can be embarrassing to admit that your school starter is not quite there yet.

Kids who still wear pull-ups might not often get a mention at school orientation days, but trust me, you're probably not the only parent in the room whose child is still wearing them on the first day of school. In fact, according to the Continence Foundation of Australia, between 3 per cent and 12 per cent of children over the age of five have problems with day-wetting, and 1 to 3 per cent struggle with faecal incontinence or soiling. The majority of these are boys.[12]

SKIPPING TO THE LOO ISN'T ALWAYS EASY

There might be any number of reasons for your child's toileting struggles, and if you haven't already sought advice from a medical professional, now might be the time to do so. Your child's reluctance to use the loo might be a physical issue, or it could be a behavioural response to sensory or emotional situations.

Perhaps one of the following reasons is a factor that you've considered but haven't sought advice about yet.

---

12   Continence Foundation of Australia, October 2013, 'Incontinence in Children: Information for Teachers Factsheet', accessed 26 January 2018, https://www.continence.org.au/pages/children.html.

Constipation

Did you know that up to 25 per cent of kids struggle with constipation?[13] I don't want to alarm you, but if this becomes a chronic problem, it can cause the bowel to stretch and that can have long-term implications for your child's wellbeing.

If constipation is affecting your child, your son's or daughter's bowel may be less sensitive than other kids of the same age. Accidents might happen because their body doesn't sense the need to go to the toilet before it's too late, leading to feelings of embarrassment and shame. If your child is affected in this way, they might also find that going to the toilet is actually painful, so it's probably understandable they would do what they can to avoid something that hurts.

If this is happening to your child, ignoring the problem could cause ongoing health issues, so it would be wise to visit your family doctor. The solutions may be simpler than you imagine. Make a diary of all your child's bowel actions and accidents for a couple of weeks and take this with you to your child's appointment. Your GP will understand your worry, and will be able to work out if taking your child to see a paediatrician or paediatric gastroenterologist for further testing and help is appropriate.

Sensory issues

Some children who have sensory processing issues are frightened by the sudden noise the toilet makes when it flushes and so prefer to avoid bathrooms altogether. For them, the tactile sensation of a snug and tightly fitting nappy or pull-up might also be preferable to cotton undies or the rough, raspy feeling of toilet paper. If your child is over-responsive or under-responsive to the senses that make our bodies function efficiently – vision, hearing, smell, touch and

---

13   Continence Foundation of Australia 2018, 'Children: Soiling', accessed 26 January 2018, https://www.continence.org.au/pages/soiling.html.

taste – they might struggle to register sensations which require no conscious thought such as thirst, hunger and the need to use their bowels. An occupational therapist who treats children with sensory processing difficulties might be able to help you with simple strategies to making going to the toilet easier for your child.

Difficult experiences

If physical causes of your child's toileting issues have been ruled out, could there be something that has happened to your son or daughter that is contributing to the problem? Sometimes, children who are feeling uncertain because of changes at home can regress to earlier stages of toileting mastery. Could a new baby, new house or even conflict between parents be affecting the dynamic at your house? Frequent accidents may be an effective, but not necessarily positive, way of gaining your attention in these kinds of situations. Similarly, your child might be reluctant to go to the toilet if he or she has had a fright while they were in a public restroom, such as being accidentally locked in a cubicle or approached by a stranger who made them feel unsafe. If you think a circumstance like this might be a factor, talk to your doctor or a psychologist about strategies you can use to help your child overcome their fear.

SCHOOL READINESS TIPS THAT YOU'VE PROBABLY NEVER HEARD BEFORE

If toileting is an issue you are worrying about, here's a few survival strategies you can start to use now and also put in place next year when school begins.

Let's start with public toilets

Public toilets, you say? What on earth have public toilets got to do with school readiness?

Well, public toilets are often very similar to the school toilets that will soon become a part of your child's life, and let me tell you, knowing how to use school toilets will be important, especially in those first weeks of school when everything is new and unfamiliar.

As adults, we often take bathroom and toilet routines for granted, but at the start of every school year teachers meet many children who worry about having an 'accident' or who simply 'hang on' until the end of the day because they don't know how to manage bathrooms at 'big school'.

Trust me – you will not want your child to be one of these kids.

At school, your child will need to be able to use cubicles with confidence. That includes being able to go into the toilet on their own, as well as locking and unlocking the door. Understanding the etiquette of not peering under the dividers between stalls will be something you might need to explain a few times too.

Your child will need to be able to confidently pull underwear down and pull it back up again, and if your child is a boy, he'll need to know how to use a urinal. Managing layers of winter clothing like stockings, as well as zips and buttons, could be something your child will need to get used to, and hygiene routines like flushing and washing hands are, of course, super important too.

Taking your child to public toilets now will provide opportunities to practise these skills while you are on hand to help. If some parts of the routine prove to be tricky for your child, you have plenty of time to teach and encourage your son or daughter before the pressure is on to get it right next year.

So, in the weeks and months before your child heads off to school, remember this tip that's lovingly given from a 'mature' teacher who's met her fair of share school starters: seek out the clean and safe public loos in your area and get your child comfortable with bathrooms

that are not the same as the one you have at home. The confidence your son or daughter will gain from practising self-help skills such as toileting will be a major advantage when 'big school' begins.

A pair and a spare

Plastic zip-lock bags might not be the most environmentally friendly way to pack a sandwich, but they are a great back-up option for storing small items in school bags.

Ask any primary school teacher and they will tell you that little kids have toileting accidents at school all the time. Some children become so engrossed in what they're doing that they don't want to pause for a pee. Others take time to learn how to put up their hand and ask to leave the room so that they can go to the toilet, or they simply leave it too late to get from the classroom to the loos in time.

It happens. And when it does, the spare pair of undies and socks that live in a zip-lock bag in your child's backpack will be a godsend. (You might be wondering why I recommend a spare pair of socks too. Well, when undies get wet, socks often do too. It's just the law of gravity when applied to a five year old.)

Next year, this seemingly innocuous zip-lock bag will do double duty if and when it's needed. Not only will it contain the clean undies and wipes that are ready for use in the case of an emergency, but it will also provide a receptacle into which used knickers can be sent home for washing.

But having emergency undies in their bag and knowing what to do with them are two different things. In the coming months before school begins, I encourage you to practise using 'a pair and a spare' with your child.

If you haven't already started giving your child a small backpack to wear when you go out together, as I suggested earlier in the book, now is the time to begin. Not only will the backpack start to teach your child about looking after his or her own belongings, but it can also house all sorts of useful items that once weighed your handbag down. Drink bottles, hats, light jackets and a favourite book or toy can all live in your child's backpack, and in a side pocket, their zip-lock bag with its spare pair of undies can go along for every ride too.

It might seem a bit far-fetched to suggest that your child learn how to change their underpants in a bathroom that's not their own, but if your child struggles with toileting, you'll probably recognise that this is not a silly suggestion at all.

The more prepared your child is for mishaps, the less upset they will be if they occur. The calm, matter-of-fact approach you take to helping them manage their unique need will be the key.

Zip-lock bags, wipes and a backpack that goes everywhere with your child – give it a try now and help your child get comfortable with the concept before school begins.

You won't regret it.

Time it right

One way to help your child get used to using the toilet on a regular (pardon the pun) basis is to create good routines around the timing of visits to the bathroom.

At school next year, your child will have a mid-morning or 'recess' break that will usually happen between 10.30 am and 11.00 am. School lunch breaks usually take place any time between 12.30 pm and 1.00 pm. If your child last went to the toilet before they left home at 8.30 am that's actually quite a long time between pit stops.

At school, the boys' and girls' toilets may become crowded at recess and lunch times. If you think your child will avoid using the loos

when other kids are around, having a home toilet routine that complements timings at school will be a good way to avoid embarrassing accidents next year.

Of course, you don't need to wait until school starts to help your child get into the habit of going to the toilet several times a day, and because little children usually respond well to predictable routines, the earlier you introduce them the better.

Some helpful times for your child to head to the bathroom might be:

- as soon as they get up in the morning
- before they go outside to play
- before they get into the car
- before a meal (this helps develop hand washing habits too)
- as soon as they arrive at a new place that has taken more than an hour to travel to
- any time when they may not be able to access a toilet for an hour or more (for example, at a cinema or airport)
- before they get into a bath, shower or pool
- before they go to bed.

Because children follow the lead set by their parents, you can be a good role model by showing your child that you go to the loo at these times too.

Stand and deliver

I once snuck into the men's loo at a swanky establishment to take a quick look at a famously ornate, gold-plated urinal. I hasten to add that a) this happened a very long time ago, b) a girlfriend dared me to do it, and c) no gentlemen were using the facility at the time.

As a female, I must admit to never having personally used a urinal, however I am the mother of a boy, and therefore you perhaps already know where I am going here.

Maybe, like me, you can attest to the delights of sharing a bathroom with the other half of our species. Perhaps you appreciate the intricacies of trying to teach junior members of that other half to use a toilet in a socially acceptable and, shall I say, hygienic manner. Next year, your son will have the unique pleasure of using the boys' toilets when he starts school. I describe it this way because as a young teacher I worked at an all-boys school and my classroom was within aromatic range of the toilet block frequented by students.

Enough said.

At home, you have possibly already used some of the tactics that mums and dads use to teach their sons how to 'stand and deliver' when they are going to the toilet. You may have used tape on the floor to help your son know where to stand so that he can judge the distance between his body and the toilet bowl. You might have discovered a new use for colourful breakfast cereals like fruit loops, which offer a biodegradable target when placed in the water. Stickers, reward charts and Buzz Lightyear underpants may all have been in your repertoire, and a new way of 'watering the garden' may have formed part of the instruction given by your son's dad and other trusted males in the family as your little boy has learned how to use the loo.

But boys' toilets at school are an entity unto themselves. There are rules and conventions a young man is expected to know, and while we probably all have a toilet anecdote that makes us smile, helping little boys who struggle with toileting get ready for the demands of school is no laughing matter. Not only are there physical, sensory

and emotional issues to deal with, but there are other logistics as well, such as how to get in and out of the toilet without wearing your own (or anyone else's) wee, when to use a cubicle, and how far to pull one's pants down.

As I said, I've never used a urinal, but American teacher Roger Torbert has. Roger's blog *Too Much to Think… Snapshots from the Life of an Aspiring Good Man* shares insights on many things, including the advice he gave to a group of five to eight year old boys about using the toilets at school in 2010. Roger's description of what boys need to know, detailed in his article *Boys – Use Your Power for Good Not Evil*, is priceless. He has kindly given his permission for me to share an excerpt with you because I couldn't have put it better myself.

Important things to remember when you go to the bathroom (by Mr Torbert):[14]

Urinals (aka – the ones on the wall)

- Stand as close to the urinal as you can before you begin to pee. Under no circumstances should you stand far back and attempt to see how far you can pee – this is something that you do in your backyard or on camping trips with your dad.

- You should make every effort to aim for the bullseye that has been placed inside the urinal. If you are peeing on the bullseye, you are likely not to be peeing on the floor.

- While standing at the urinal, you are not to turn to the left or right to check out what others are doing. Reason #1: you don't want people to look at you while you are peeing and they don't want you to look at them while they are peeing. Reason #2: when you are looking to the side, you are not concentrating on the bullseye and could turn your entire body to the left or right 'mid pee'.

---

14 Reprinted with the kind permission of Roger Torbert.

- There is no need to drop your pants to your ankles while standing at the urinal – no one needs to see your butt.

- Only one person at a time at each urinal. Stand in line and wait your turn.

- If you are waiting in line to use the urinal, DO NOT drop your pants to get ready for your turn – wait until you are actually at the urinal before unbuttoning your pants.

- Do not sit in urinal – it is for standing only. If you need to sit, please use the toilet.

- Those blue things are called urinal cakes – they are not edible and should not be removed from the urinal for any reason.

Toilet (aka – the ones you sit on)

- It is alright to stand up in front of the toilet to pee – boys are very lucky to be able to stand up to pee. Use this power for good and not evil.

- Only one person at a time at each toilet. Stand in line and wait your turn.

- There is no bullseye in the toilet – aim for the hole in the bottom or just aim for the water (making bubbles can be fun).

- Raise the seat before you begin to pee. If you pee on the seat and don't clean it up, the next person who has to sit down to poop will have to sit in your pee. Do you want to sit in someone else's pee?

- If you do accidental pee on the seat, clean it up. Use the 'just right' amount of toilet paper to do this. Use more than 1–2 squares because you don't want to get pee on your hands. Don't use a huge amount because it will clog the toilet and folks won't be able to poop when they need to.

- After cleaning the seat, be sure to wash your hands.
- If you are sitting on the toilet and someone looks under the stall (or over it), tell them to leave you alone and tell your teacher as soon as you get back to your class room.

Drain in the Floor (Drain in the Floor)

- The drain in the bathroom floor is not for pee. You should not stand around this hole to pee with your friends.

Using the toilet at school is likely to be a daily occurrence for your child for the next decade and beyond, so building your child's independence (and in some cases, courage) in the bathroom could be a priority for you right now. If you need professional help, I encourage you to seek it before your child's sensitivities start to impact their confidence and self-care skills. Toileting troubles are commonly supported by family GPs and the Continence Foundation of Australia, which offers excellent free resources for families. A local occupational therapist or psychologist may be able to assist you with customised strategies that meet your child's personal needs too.

CHAPTER 13

HOW TO HELP A FUSSY EATER

'Before Alexander started school, I estimated that there were only about twenty foods that I could be confident he would eat. I lost count of the number of times I was told that he would eat when he was hungry. I knew that people meant well, but they just didn't get it. Alexander's sensory reactions to food were so strong that nothing on earth would encourage him to try a food if he was afraid of it. Dinnertime was a battle every night and anything to do with food was stressful for him and for me. Before he went to school, I knew that he wouldn't learn or behave well if he was hungry. I worried about what on earth I could put in his lunchbox that he might be tempted to eat and hoped that his fussy habits wouldn't get in the way of him making friends.'

Helena, Alexander's mum

Helena's son Alexander has always been a fussy eater. A fan of bland foods such as white rice, pasta, cheese and yoghurt, he still steadfastly refuses to eat most meats, and gags when the smell, taste or texture of a food is too much for him. Having endured two years of preschool where Alexander rarely ate anything that was offered to him by teachers and the on-site cook, Helena was very stressed about how his fussy eating would affect him when he started school.

If your child, like Helena's, is a fussy eater, you've no doubt sought advice from a range of experts and tried all of the tips known to man in an effort to expand your son's or daughter's food repertoire.

I know. It's hard, and I've been there too.

FOOD FIGHTS

Before my son started school, I worried that my fussy eater wasn't getting the nutrition he needed to grow and thrive. I took him to doctors and specialists, who looked at the food diary I kept and assured me that the small number of foods he was prepared to eat were healthy, but that didn't allay the fears of a mum whose four year old's diet consisted of bland foods and anything that resembled a chicken nugget.

Food caused constant conflict at our house, and I could see that our focus on whether our son would eat or not was stressing him out. It wasn't great for my blood pressure either. I wished that my child's mealtime choices didn't dominate our lives, but they did. For years. And because of them, the places we could go and the things we could do together as a family were limited. Perhaps you can relate. Many parents describe their child as being a 'fussy eater' because, on occasion, their child won't eat what is offered to them or throws a tantrum at the dinner table. There might be lots of reasons for this, including sincerely not being a fan of the menu or simply being too tired to sit still and use a knife and fork at the end of a long day. You know this, of course, and if your child's feeding issues go beyond the occasional mealtime meltdown, you've probably been looking for solutions for your child's fussy eating for a while.

SENDING OUT AN SOS

My own search for answers has led me to the work of paediatric psychologist Dr Kay Toomey, the developer of the SOS (Sequential Oral Sensory) Approach to Feeding. Dr Toomey believes that there is a difference between a 'picky eater' and a 'problem eater'. If you are worried about your child's food intake at school next year, it might be helpful for you to look into her work.

In a nutshell, the SOS Approach to Feeding is based on the idea that eating is the most challenging sensory skill children have to master. As parents of fussy eaters, we tend to focus on food quite a lot because we worry about what and how we are going to get our child to eat today. However, Dr Toomey says the pressure we put on our child to eat can cause them to feel stressed. Unfortunately, when a child is stressed, their body releases adrenalin. Adrenalin is an appetite suppressant, so when our stressed-out fussy eaters tell us they are not hungry, this may indeed be true. Instead of being in the relaxed 'learning' mode that's needed to experiment and try new foods at mealtimes, their bodies go into a defensive 'react' mode that makes them fear and resist foods which have unfamiliar flavours, smells and textures. And that's where the battles begin.

If I'd known about the SOS Approach when my son was little, I would have jumped on it because, in our case, it just makes sense. My guy is much older now, but he's still quite particular about what he will eat. Some of my colleagues at Kids First Children's Services are now trained in the SOS Approach to Feeding, and the things I have learned from them have certainly changed the way I now deal with breakfasts, lunchboxes and evening meals.

When you have a fussy eater, it can be hard to know where to start or who to turn to, so if you've never heard of the SOS Approach to Feeding, I encourage you to check it out to see if it resonates with you and your family. It is a family-focused, developmental approach to help children learn to eat a wider range of foods, and you will find quite a lot of information about it on the internet. There may also be a speech pathologist or occupational therapist in your area who is trained to deliver it. You never know – the barriers that are standing in the way of your child's mealtime behaviour might not be as insurmountable as they seem, and if you're able to try some new strategies now, recess and lunchtime may be less of a drama than you fear next year.

HOW TO FEED YOUR FUSSY EATER AT SCHOOL

Before worries about what your child is going to eat at school start to keep you awake at night, may I share a few things I have learned over many years of packing lunchboxes for a child who was – and to be honest, still is – a fussy eater?

Familiar foods are your friend

Recess and lunchtime are full of things that will bombard your child's sensory system. If your son or daughter is very sensitive to the smell, taste and texture of food, it's quite possible that he or she will find the noise, action and unpredictability of the playground demanding to deal with too.

If you send your reluctant eater to school with a lunchbox that's full of new and unfamiliar foods, there's a very high chance that it will come home untouched, because there's only so much that a sensory-sensitive child can process at one time. If you really want to ensure that your child will eat at school, leave learning about new foods for home and send to school foods that he or she won't think twice about eating.

It's okay to send the same thing every day

At the start of the year, the media seems to saturate us with advice from master chefs and super mums who promote the idea that every day's school lunchbox should be full of delicious, diverse and different culinary delights. Don't get sucked in to the hype or feel that you are a failure because your child thrives on routine. My son ate cream-cheese sandwiches every day for years, and because he knew that this was a safe food, lunchtime stress didn't add to the social and emotional demands of his school day. Remember, the aim of the game is to ensure your child eats *something* at recess and lunchtime. Send the same thing every day if that's what works for your sensitive child. None of the other five year olds will be looking into your son's or daughter's lunchbox to give it a score out of ten.

Mealtime myths

For some reason, our culture has some fairly rigid ideas about what foods are appropriate to eat at certain times of the day. Have you ever asked yourself why we think it's okay to eat processed cereal or toast at 7.00 am, but options such as rice, pasta, chicken and fish are only appropriate after noon?

Early in my son's school journey I learned the value of letting him eat foods he liked at breakfast time, and this was reinforced in his final years of high school when stress affected his appetite. Regardless of whether he was at preschool, primary school or high school, his days were full of demanding new experiences. My sensitive son would be emotionally exhausted by the end of the day, and so introducing difficult new foods at dinnertime was a recipe for disaster. In contrast, he was fresh in the mornings, and so this became a

good time to give him highly nutritious, filling foods that weren't too threatening. Perhaps this is a strategy that you could try too.

I became the queen of potato fritters bumped up with tuna or mashed cannellini beans, egg milkshakes, and toasted sandwiches. They were filling and nutritious and, more importantly, my fussy eater loved them. They sometimes took a little bit more time to prepare than throwing cornflakes into a bowl, but so what? It was a win for him and a win for me because he went to school with a full tummy, feeling calm and ready to face the day. If your child eats more easily in the morning, let go of mealtime myths and do what works. There really isn't any such thing as a 'breakfast food', 'lunch food' or 'dinner food'.

Who said you have to send sandwiches?

Do you remember eating warm, squashed sandwiches that, while lovingly packed in a brown paper bag or simple plastic lunchbox, just didn't survive the hours they spent in your schoolbag? Me too. These days, we are spoiled for choice when it comes to lunchboxes, and this is great news for your fussy eater. The advent of insulated containers and lunch bags means that it's easier than it's ever been to send the kinds of foods your child will eat to school. If your child likes yoghurt, crumbed chicken fingers or homemade sausage rolls that you've secretly stuffed with grated veggies, you're in luck. Insulated bags and ice bricks that last for hours are easily available in all shapes and sizes, and could be a godsend for you as they have been for me.

At my house, my husband is the king of lunchboxes. On weekends, he often prepares batches of favourites like pies, schnitzel strips, crumbed potato cakes and sausage rolls in advance, so he can then freeze them in individual portions. They last for weeks, and this strategy certainly makes it easy to put a lunchbox together on busy mornings when everyone is in a hurry. The food thaws during the morning so that it's fresh and ready to eat, and in winter you'd be surprised at how effective aluminium foil and an insulated bag are for keeping hot foods warm too.

In the next few months, you might like to try these options with your child. Instead of waiting for the January sales, buy your child's lunchbox now and use it as often as you can. Not only will your child benefit from the opportunity to practise their fine motor skills by opening and closing their lunchbox, but you will get the chance to test-run foods that your son or daughter will and won't eat. This will take some of the worry and guesswork out of starting school, because at least you'll know that the food you send to school has a good chance of being consumed.

Five's the limit

I know. You have a fussy eater and so you're tempted to send lots of different foods to school in the hope that your son or daughter will eat at least one of them. You might be thinking, *'If he doesn't eat the bread roll, then at least he might try the mini-pie,'* or, *'If she doesn't want the muffin, maybe she'll eat the fruit pack'*.

As a teacher who's done plenty of playground duty and a mum who's seen many a lunchbox come home half full, please believe me when I tell you that most children don't unpack everything in their school bag if they are faced with lots of separate boxes and containers.

For a fussy eater, too many options is simply overwhelming. Kids stress over whether mum or dad is going to comment on what they did and didn't eat when they get home, and rummaging through multiple packets of food is also time consuming. At recess and lunchtime, most children's main priority is to socialise with friends, so don't expect that difficult to access food will win in a competition with play.

These days, bento-box-style lunchboxes which have partitioned sections and a spot for an ice brick are a great option for all kids, and especially fussy eaters. I suggest that you pack a maximum of five alternatives, and that you always ensure there are some nutritious, tried-and-true favourites which you know your child likes. This style of lunchbox will give your child choice over what they eat and when they eat it, and this is important for fussy eaters who sometimes feel pressured at mealtimes.

A word of warning though… make sure your child knows how to secure the lock on the box. Bento boxes are great because they reduce the need for environmentally unfriendly packaging, but the moment your child leaves their lunchbox unsecured, you'll know it. There's nothing like retrieving squashed banana and rogue sultanas from the deepest, darkest crevices of a school bag to let you know that you are now the parent of a big school kid.

ASK TEACHERS TO BE YOUR ALLY

If your child is a very fussy eater, it's helpful to let the classroom teacher know. In most Australian schools, children bring their lunch with them to school and eat it in a designated part of the playground. Many schools have a 'first half' of lunch with an allocated time in which children are required to sit and eat before a bell rings to announce the start of play time. The school your child goes to next year may or may not have these routines in place, so it is probably wise to ask so that you can prepare your child accordingly. Some ideas for this kind of practice include sitting outside to eat lunch when you are at home or taking your child (and their lunchbox) to the park where they learn to eat first and then play.

Sometimes, well-meaning teachers who are only trying to help may be perceived by your child as the 'food police'. This happens if teachers frequently comment on the limited selection of foods in their lunchbox, or the speed at which they are eating. Some schools also require children to show the teacher on duty their empty lunchbox before they are allowed to go and play. This can mean that the birds and other wildlife who live in the vicinity have a smorgasbord of daily treats when uneaten lunches are secreted in garden beds by five year olds who know that if they don't get rid of their leftovers, they will be made to eat everything in their lunchbox and therefore miss out on playtime.

If any aspect of the way your child's school manages recess and lunchtime meals concerns you, a quick email or phone call to the teacher to explain where your child is up to might be helpful. You might say or write something like:

> *Thank you so much for your support and interest as Harry learns to eat new foods. As you know, our family is working hard to help him become a more adventurous eater. At the moment, we are introducing new foods at home and providing him with familiar foods to eat at school so that he builds confidence. Our at-home approach also includes not commenting on his food choices or the time it takes him to eat. We are finding that this helps him to cope better with eating, which is a process he finds very demanding. If you have any concerns or would like to chat to me about the food I am sending to school for Harry to eat at recess and lunchtime, please feel free to give me a call. Again, thanks so much for your understanding …*

TRY NOT TO TALK ABOUT IT

I get it. You'll have been worried all day about whether your fussy eater ate anything at preschool or school. Naturally, it's one of the first questions you want to ask your child when you arrive to take them home, and before you leave you may even ask the teacher too.

Finding out what your child did and didn't eat is very important to you, and so for you, inspecting their lunchbox the moment you get home might be a priority too.

Here's the thing: the attention we parents place on food and the fear of disappointing us can make our fussy eaters more anxious. As we know, anxiety can be an appetite suppressant, and that's the last thing sensitive kids who struggle with feeding need.

If you can, try to manage your own worries about your child's eating by not making it the focus of your conversation at the end of the day. After all, your child has probably enjoyed lots of fun and valuable learning experiences with their friends and teacher. Sharing those with your child is probably more important than whether they ate their muffin, right?

It's hard to pretend that your child's lunchbox doesn't matter, but if you can reduce the importance you give it, you will give your son or daughter a vital message. You're telling them that what they did and how they felt that day is what you're most interested in. You can always check the lunchbox out when your child is not around, but remember, do what you can to take the emotion out of what your child ate at school. The last thing your fussy eater needs to feel is they have let you down.

GET HELP IF YOU NEED IT

Having a fussy eater is stressful, and if you have one, you are not alone. The earlier you start getting ready for big school the better, so break out that new lunchbox and have a think about what you are serving and when. If the range of foods your child is prepared to eat is worrying you, seek professional advice. There's only so much you can do alone, but with the support and guidance of someone who is experienced and trained to help, you might be surprised at the progress your child could make before school begins. Your family doctor might be a good place to start to ensure that your child's difficulties are not medically based. A dentist could check if your child's mouth, teeth and jaw are developing appropriately, and a speech pathologist or occupational therapist with specific training in feeding may also be able to assist.

CHAPTER 14

HOW TO MANAGE MELTDOWNS

'Taj's meltdowns are exhausting, not just for him, but for everyone around him too. Before he started school, I was terrified that he was going to be labelled as the naughty boy because when he is overwhelmed he just can't cope in the way that other kids do. For a while everything can go along calmly, but if a noise is too loud or a child accidentally touches him while they are lining up to go into the classroom, he can lose the plot in the blink of an eye. When I take him to the park, I have to be on high alert in case he lashes out at other kids who aren't playing the way he wants them to, and so you can imagine how worried I was about how he would go in the playground at school.'

Kristy, Taj's mum

Like many kids with sensory processing difficulties, Kristy's son, Taj, has always been a boy with a need for speed. Rarely able to sit still and always on the go, Taj is the kind of child whose responses to sensory inputs such as loud noises, unexpected physical contact and 'big' feelings like disappointment or excitement have caused challenges at home and preschool since he was a very young child.

I've met many children like Taj in both my professional and personal lives, and if your child's emotional and social reactions to sensory stimuli are unpredictable you might resonate with Kristy's uncertain feelings as your child prepares to start school.

Let's be honest: it can be extremely difficult to be the parent of a child whose explosive behaviour affects their learning and relationships. On the surface, their sensory reactions can look like wilful, rebellious behaviour to people who don't know them well. You might be one of the many parents to whom well-meaning friends and family have contributed unsolicited advice about creating boundaries. You may also have been on the receiving end of comments from complete strangers who have made unfair judgements about your parenting skills when your child has had a public meltdown.

The reality is that children with sensory processing sensitivities need support, not judgement, so in this chapter, let's look at why your child might be experiencing these intense reactions and some practical things you can do to build your child's coping skills as they head off to school.

But before I do that, allow me to share an analogy that may put this concept into some perspective. It's one that I have shared with thousands of parents and teachers who have heard me speak at seminars or met me at Kids First Children's Services. While it's by no means a medically accurate explanation of the way children's brains and bodies cope with the world around them, many parents have told me that this version makes better sense to them than the jargon-filled descriptions of kids' proprioceptive and vestibular systems that they've read or heard before.

YOUR CHILD'S BRAIN IS STILL ON ITS 'L' PLATES

Without getting too scientific or medical on you, the analogy starts with understanding how your child's brain works.

Research has shown that your child's brain will not develop fully until they are in their mid-twenties, so it stands to reason that your five year old's brain is still on its 'L' plates and has a long way to go before it is functioning at its full potential.[15]

The brain is an incredibly complicated thing, but in the simplest of terms it has three main sections, and these 'drive' your child's thoughts, feelings, actions and reactions:

1. The 'ancient' part of the brain that is closest to the spinal cord drives their instinctive functions, like breathing. It controls the things your child does without thinking.

2. The 'limbic' system that runs across the middle of your child's brain drives not only the behaviours they need for survival, such as feeding and reproduction, but also their hormones and the emotions that are associated with their 'fight or flight response'. (Hold onto this idea, because I will come back to it!)

3. The 'frontal' lobe area of the brain is where the 'pre-frontal cortex' lives. It's this part of the brain that does the heavy lifting when it comes to making decisions, planning and considering consequences. This is the part of the brain that

---

15   Johnson, Sara B et al., 'Adolescent Maturity and the Brain: the promise and pitfalls of neuroscience research in adolescent health policy', *Journal of Adolescent Health*, Volume 45, Issue 3, 216–221.

takes a long time to develop into full maturity, and this may explain why so many grown-ups can tell tales of the silly things they did when they were adolescents.

Still with me? Good!

Psychiatrist Dr Daniel Siegel and educator Tina Payne Bryson explain this next concept beautifully in their book *The Whole-Brain Child: 12 Revolutionary strategies to nurture your child's developing mind*.[16] If you are interested, their explanation of this idea is no doubt much better than mine, however when your child's brain is affected by stimulus that makes them react in an emotional manner, the connection with the 'thinking' part of their brain is disrupted.

The limbic system takes over, and so for children who struggle with sensory processing, moments of fear, frustration, disappointment or even high excitement can mean their brain forgets about socially appropriate reactions, and their bodies just do what feels right.

This may mean a child who is hyper-sensitive to noises, tastes or smells might do everything possible to *avoid* those things if they find them confronting (hello, fussy eaters!). And it may mean that kids who are hypo-sensitive to stimuli, like movement, do more than is usual to *seek* these sensations out so that their body and brain can be in sync (welcome to the party, kids who can't sit still!).

With this understanding of how our sensitive children's brains and bodies work, perhaps it's easier to understand why our kids with sensory processing difficulties behave in the way they do.

When their 'fight or flight' instinct kicks in, all sorts of avoidance strategies start, and that's what we see when they melt down or resist the things that don't seem to bother their peers. (See, I told you I'd come back to that idea!)

---

16 Siegel, DJ & Bryson, TP (2011). *The Whole-Brain Child: 12 revolutionary strategies to nurture your child's developing mind*. New York: Delacorte Press.

KIDS ARE LIKE A CUP

So… understanding that your sensitive child's brain is always reacting to internal and external sensations, let me introduce another idea.

And that is that kids are like a cup.

Every day, their bodies and brains 'fill' with the sights, sounds, touches, tastes, smells and feelings that they are exposed to.

Some children's cups fill very slowly, but others have a fast-filling cup, and if lots of stimuli flows into it all at once, it overflows. When that happens to your child, the 'thinking' part of their brain (the pre-frontal cortex) is 'flooded' by the chemicals that the limbic system produces. The 'sensible' part of their brain disengages, allowing emotion and instinct to take over.

And that's when a meltdown can occur.

If you have ever tried to comfort an overwhelmed child whose 'cup' has 'overflowed', you'll know that it's almost impossible for them to see reason or to think logically when they are in that heightened emotional state. A tantrum or meltdown might take a long time to subside, and it could feel like forever until your child is able to think rationally again.

But it's not just children who struggle to think clearly and act appropriately when emotion takes over.

When was the last time you had a 'robust' conversation with someone you love about an issue you felt strongly about? Did you stay calm and cool, or did you lose the plot?

How long did it take for you to calm down and be able to see things with perspective?

Little kids who struggle with sensory processing face these kinds of challenges often. You might recognise this in your sensitive child, who – like a meerkat – is often hyper-vigilant and anxious in environments that cause their cups to fill quickly.

Sometimes this sensory defensiveness can lead to avoidant behaviours than can be hard for the rest of us to understand, and there's no doubt that such behaviours get in the way of children's learning and relationships when they are misunderstood or not managed well.

MANIC MORNINGS

Mornings are often the time when kids with sensory processing difficulties begin to struggle. In busy households, where the going-to-school-and-work routine requires everyone to get their act together and leave home by a certain time, there's always the potential for a meltdown if your sensitive child becomes overwhelmed.

For kids with sensory processing challenges, emotions can escalate very quickly to that 'my cup is full and ready to overflow' state if repeated requests to get dressed, brush their teeth, find their shoes and get into the car are made loudly by frustrated parents whose increasing levels of emotion project onto their sensitive child.

Is it any wonder that these little ones, whose 'cups' are so full, melt down when the emotional demand of being separated from their mum or dad presents at the school gate?

The behaviour they are demonstrating is not wilfulness.

For the sensitive child with sensory processing difficulties, it's overwhelm.

STRATEGIES TO MANAGE MELTDOWNS

Every day, I work with highly trained occupational therapists who support children with sensory processing difficulties. Sometimes it's hard to explain what they do, and that's why I came up with this 'kids are like a cup' analogy.

Ideally, the aim for children who are very sensitive to sights, sounds, touches, tastes, smells and feelings is to keep their cup at 'half full' so that, when a social, emotional or learning demand comes their way, they are able to cope and avoid a situation in which their cup overflows.

To give you another analogy that I share with seminar guests, it's a little bit like driving a car.

As an experienced driver, you can no doubt drive and sing along with the radio at the same time. You are calm, but you are alert – so if a ball, dog or even a child crosses your path, you are hopefully able to hit the brakes and stop the car in time.

In this scenario, because you were calm, but still alert, you managed the unexpected demand that came your way, and because of that you were successful in doing what you needed to do.

This state of being 'calm, but alert' is technically known as 'regulation'.

All children, and in fact all people, need to feel regulated to deal with the demands of their daily lives, but for kids with sensory processing difficulties, this can take a little more conscious planning than for the rest of us.

The great news about kids with sensory processing challenges is that, with the right support, they can learn to keep their cup at half full. And when their cup is only half full, they are less likely to melt down and more likely to be able to do the things other kids take for granted, like learning, making friends and enjoying new experiences.

PUTTING A DRAIN IN YOUR CHILD'S CUP

This has been a long route to the solutions I promised you at the start of this chapter, but hopefully the background information you have just read will give you a better understanding of why your sensory-sensitive child struggles with so many seemingly simple things.

The key now is to know how to *keep* your child's cup at half full so that they are better able to manage the demands of their day.

In my experience, this is where occupational therapists with post-graduate training in sensory processing come into their own. They have a deep understanding of how children's sensory systems work, and if you find a good OT, you might find that you can make a world of difference to your child's chances of school success next year, and more importantly, to your family right now.

Occupational therapists who work in this area are trained to identify the specific things that contribute to your child's meltdowns, and can help you to implement an easy but effective 'sensory diet' of daily two-minute activities that reduce the levels of arousal that are filling your child's 'cup'.

The key is to think of these strategies as *pre-emptive* ones.

There's no point implementing sensory support for a child who has already melted down. Our objective is to help your child avoid meltdowns altogether, and so that means strategies need to be put into place *before* your child heads into a situation that is challenging.

It's a bit like making sure you have something to eat before you go to a party where alcoholic drinks will be served. To avoid things getting 'messy', you prepare before you leave home.

If you think of your child's sensory needs as a constant party that they need to 'prep' for, you'll be heading in the right direction.

Strategies to support your child's sensory processing

There are some key approaches that occupational therapists draw on when they are developing a sensory diet for sensory-sensitive children who are prone to having meltdowns.

These include:

- *Deep pressure activities:* Deep pressure refers to a form of tactile (touch) input, and often children who struggle with sensory processing find it very calming. Does your child like big hugs, 'squishes' or wearing tightly fitting clothing such as leggings? These may be ways in which your child is trying to keep their body regulated, so talk to an OT about the kinds of calming deep-pressure activities that could support your child's social and emotional regulation.

- *Heavy work:* This involves tasks that 'activate' your child's confidence about where their body is in space (the technical term for this is 'proprioception'). For many kids who struggle with sensory processing, activities that give them the opportunity to use the large muscles in their body to pull, push or lift something can be very calming. Think about adults who love to go to the gym to do a weights session before they go to work. It's the same concept. When we use our muscles well, we help our brain to get set for the challenges that come our way. An OT who can advise you about the right proprioceptive activities to inject into your child's routine could make a big difference to your child's behavioural success.

- *Oral motor strategies:* Oral motor input is more than our taste buds. The mouth, tongue and jaw can also provide lots of proprioceptive input to your child's body through tasks such as chewing and sucking. Many sensory-sensitive kids calm their bodies by putting things in their mouths. This might be familiar to you if your child chews on non-food items or pieces of clothing such as sleeves, hat cords and collars. Again, an occupational therapist can help you with strategies so your child can meet this sensory need in a socially appropriate way.

- *Respiration activities:* Respiration refers to our breath, and breathing plays an important role in helping your child's body to feel calm. Think about the last time someone told you to take a deep breath so that you could focus on something that was hard to do. It could have been anything from a difficult yoga pose to managing the demands of childbirth or even dealing with someone who has had a shock after a car accident. Breathing activities are a great way to help sensory-sensitive kids manage their emotions. One of the positives aspects of respiration strategies is that, once they are learned, they can be become a life-long tactic to use in moments of escalation or stress.

- *Vestibular input:* I've tried to keep this as jargon-free as possible, but vestibular input is the sense of movement that is centred in our inner ear. Spinning, hanging upside down and swinging are activities that can be intensely calming for kids who are always on the move (like Taj, who we met at the start of this chapter). When children with these kinds of sensory processing needs are supported with planned movement opportunities, they have a much better chance of staying on task in classrooms. As you can imagine, the wrong kinds of vestibular inputs can make things worse instead of better for a sensory-seeking child, so an occupational therapist who is trained to deliver sensory-focused therapy is the person you should speak with about a sensory diet that includes these kinds of activities.

Times that tantrums often occur

In setting up a sensory diet for your child, it will be helpful for you to think about the times of day that are most challenging.

If the playground at recess or lunchtime is the setting for meltdowns and temper tantrums, putting some sensory diet activities in place *before* your child goes outside will put a 'drain' in their cup and give them increased capacity to manage the social and emotional demands of the noise, movement and unpredictability of the school yard.

If mornings result in intense tantrums or abject refusal to cooperate, you may need to implement some sensory support strategies for a few minutes before breakfast so that your child does not become too overwhelmed by your family's busy morning routine.

If you can take action before your child goes to the shops, a birthday party, swimming lessons or the family gathering that usually ends in tears, you are much more likely to have success. Don't forget though that if your child is in a stressful environment for a long time, they may need a pit stop to drain their cup again, so talk to your OT about strategies that are easy to implement when you are out and about.

FIND OUT WHAT WORKS FOR YOUR CHILD

Every child's sensory processing system is different, and what works for your child might not work for another. The idea, though, is to find out what your child is sensitive to, and then to work out what the 'antidote' to that sensitivity is.

The good news is that these activities do not have to take a long time out of your day, and they usually aren't difficult either.

They won't work unless you are consistent, though, so I encourage you to get good advice so that you can learn how to support your child at home and in the classroom, as well as in the playground and community.

OTHER PEOPLE WILL ONLY UNDERSTAND WHEN YOU DO

If you have a sensory-sensitive child, hopefully the explanations I have given here will provide you with the starting point you need as you begin to understand your child's behaviour.

The concepts involved in sensory processing are complex and sometimes they are not commonly understood. Sadly, it's often easier for adults to blame your child's reactive behaviour on disobedience or poor parenting than to investigate the factors that contribute to their meltdowns. That's why it's important to educate yourself about your child's sensory and behavioural needs, and to seek support from qualified professionals who can help you to become a champion for your child.

As you and your child get ready for school, remember that other people's understanding of your child starts with you. Teachers, principals and even passers-by only see part of the picture – but you have a 360-degree view of your child's needs.

At the end of this book I've listed a few resources you might like to check out so that you can more fully understand the role your child's sensory processing plays in their behaviour. The more you understand about how your child's brain and body respond to situations, the better you will be able to explain their needs to teachers at school.

So if you are the parent of a sensory-sensitive kid, hang in there!

You are definitely not alone, and there is light at the end of the meltdown and tantrum tunnel.

PART V

MAKING YOURSELF HEARD

Some parents tell me that schools and teachers make them nervous. The moment they walk in the door, memories of their own school days come flooding back and they feel intimidated and anxious, even though they are successful, independent adults now.

If your memories of your own school days, the headmaster's office and classroom struggles are less than pleasant, you might feel this way too.

Some of the trickiest things for parents to get used to at their child's primary school are the communication conventions that mums and dads are expected to know, understand and adhere to when touching base with teachers. I don't want to disappoint you, but if the person who conducted your school tour assured you that the principal's door would be 'always open', it's entirely possible that was a slight exaggeration.

Teachers are happy to talk to parents, but they just can't do it in an ad-hoc way because, if they did, they'd have no time to teach our kids. So if you're accustomed to having a daily chat with the teacher and carers at your child's current preschool, you may have to adjust your expectations next year. With hundreds of children, parents and carers coming and going every day, primary school could require a slight step out of your conversational comfort zone.

Having said that, if you've read this far in this book, I'm fairly confident you're committed to being an effective advocate for your child next year, and in all the years after that. The good news is that there are lots of ways to make sure your voice is heard and that you start your collaboration with your child's new teachers on the right foot next year. Let's take a look at what they are so that, just like your child, you are ready for the changes that being part of a primary school community will bring.

CHAPTER 15

HOW TO SPEAK UP WITHOUT SHOUTING

'During the first couple of weeks of Kindergarten, the teacher was quite available to parents after school, but once that initial period of settling in was over, she would say goodbye to the children at the end of the day and close the classroom door. It was hard for me to get used to because I'd been in the habit of having a daily catch up with Max's preschool teachers. I felt that I needed to know more so that I could keep his OT in the loop, but at times it felt like the teacher was keeping me at arm's length.'

Louise, Max's mum

Louise's son Max struggles with sensory processing. Apart from being an extremely fussy eater who will only eat buttered bread, white rice, pasta and yoghurt, he becomes easily overwhelmed in noisy and unpredictable environments. During Max's preschool years, she developed a close relationship with his early educators who collaborated frequently with Max's occupational therapist, but when school began Louise worried about how to communicate with his new teacher.

KNOWING WHERE TO BEGIN WITH TEACHERS

Louise's experience is a common one. When your sensitive child heads off to school next year, you too might find that teachers are slightly less available than you have been accustomed to.

There are lots of reasons for the changes you might notice at school. Preschool teachers usually work in an environment with a ratio of one adult to every ten children, while primary school teachers often have double that number of students in their classes. Even before teachers factor in after-school staff meetings, programming and preparation for the following day and their own parenting responsibilities, it's rarely possible for them to have a detailed daily chat with every parent who wants to talk about the intricacies of their child's day.

Don't get me wrong. Teachers *do* want to talk to you, but the secret is knowing how and when to have these conversations so that you get the outcomes you need and are able to build a healthy partnership with your child's teacher.

WHEN TO START THE CONVERSATION

The months before school begins are the best time to start a conversation with your child's new school about their unique needs. Timing is everything, so it might be helpful to remember that, from November onwards, things get a bit frantic for teachers. End-of-year reports, meetings and school events such as concerts and awards ceremonies are added to their usual workload, so if you want to talk to them about your child who's arriving next year, you're likely to get more from the meeting if you catch up with them in October.

There are probably lots of things you will want to talk about at your first meeting, but remember your time will probably be limited to a maximum of one hour. From the school's perspective, the purpose of the first meeting will be to:

- give you an opportunity to meet key teachers, and for them to meet you

- discuss the support needs your child has

- clarify what you will do, and what the school will do, to make starting school as successful as possible for your child.

Don't worry, you will have opportunities to discuss specifics later, but first things first. Teachers want to meet you and talk to you so that they can then go away and plan. They won't necessarily have all the answers in October, but if things work the way they should, they'll be ready to rock by the end of January.

WHAT TO TAKE WITH YOU

It's understandable that you will want to tell the teacher as much as you can about your child and the things that make your son or daughter special. After all, you have five years of experiences and knowledge to share. You may have folders full of reports from doctors, therapists and other professionals that you've read, highlighted and stuck post-it notes on, but if you can, try not to overwhelm teachers with paperwork when you first meet them.

Your first meeting at your child's new school is like a first date. Everyone will be on their best behaviour, and it's your first chance to give the school a sense of who you and your child are. Try not to

spoil it by turning up with 300 pieces of paper which you expect the principal and teacher to read there and then.

Of course, there may be some vital documentary evidence the principal will need if he or she is going to apply for a teacher's aide or special resources for your child. For example, if your child is gifted, you will probably be asked to provide a psychologist's testing report that is less than twelve months old. Similarly, if your child is diagnosed with a disability such as autism or cerebral palsy, you will need confirmation letters from doctors that are relatively recent.

As much as principals would love to apply for funding so that extra support can be put in place for every sensitive child with unique needs, they are constrained by the system they are part of. Don't be surprised if you are told the school has no access to extra funding for your anxious daughter or your son who has ADHD.

It might not seem fair, it might not make sense, but the system is the system. Sometimes parents don't like it, and often teachers aren't raving fans either, but if you spend your very first meeting at your child's new school focusing on negatives rather than positives, you won't make the flying start that you are hoping for.

CHAPTER 16

THE BEST TIMES TO TALK TO TEACHERS

'It's understandable that sending their child off to school is something that parents gear up for over a period of months, but it can be hard to manage the expectations they have of me at the beginning of the year. Some have a list of questions a mile long before the first day is even over, and expect that I will be able to have an hour-long meeting with them in the first week of school. At that stage of the term, I'm usually just meeting their children for the first or second time. There's only one of me, but I have the needs of 20 or more children and their families to juggle. I prefer to get to know my students a little before I have meetings with parents so that the conversations I have with them are meaningful.'

Sam, Kindergarten teacher

Sam is a popular primary school teacher who has taught Kindergarten in a Sydney school for the past three years. He says he is always happy to talk with the parents of his students, but that it can be difficult to give everyone the time and attention they need.

Sam's predicament is not uncommon, and if you are a teacher his experience may resonate with you. Situations like this happen every year in schools all over Australia, and Kindergarten teachers aren't the only ones who feel the pressure.

The first few weeks of school are a whirlwind for all teachers and students, regardless of whether they are starting school for the very first time, or returning to classrooms and playgrounds that they know well. Anxious parents, keen to make sure the teacher has their child's needs front of mind, have been known to jockey for position in the scrum of mums and dads that gathers outside the classroom at home time, or even lay in wait in the carpark so they can 'have a quick word' with their child's teacher at the start or the end of the day.

You will be keen, of course, to get to know your child's teacher, but I encourage you not to be the parent who ambushes your child's hard-working teacher. It will take time for the teacher to get to know your child and you. If you can be a little patient, you're likely to get more from a planned conversation conducted in week three than you will from a snatched doorstop debrief in week one.

PARENT–TEACHER NIGHTS

Almost all schools have a designated parent–teacher night on their annual calendars. These after-school and early-evening events can take place any time during first or second term, and will give you a ten-minute opportunity to discuss your child's learning, progress, skills and interests with the teacher. Timeframes are usually strictly adhered to, and often parents wait in a line outside the classroom for their turn to talk to the teacher. This might mean the one and only parent–teacher night of the year may not be the best occasion on which to deal with a detailed, and possibly confidential, conversation about your child's unique needs. If you need to have that kind of chat, make an appointment to see the teacher at another, mutually convenient time.

PICKING YOUR MOMENT

Busy school calendars that include concerts, camps and the writing of twice-yearly reports mean there are some times of the term that are better than others when it comes to meeting privately with teachers. Most of the teachers I know say the best time to have parent–teacher meetings is between week three and week nine of the term. This timeframe gives them the chance to gather the information you need to know about, and also be able to follow up on the things they've discussed with you before the term ends.

If you ask them to be honest, teachers will tell you there are times of day that work better for them too. While first thing in the morning might work perfectly well for your work schedule, it might not be as convenient for a teacher who has before-school staff meetings, playground duty or children of their own to wrangle between 8.00 am and 8.30 am. Similarly, teachers who have personal and professional obligations at the end of the school day might prefer to meet with you before school begins.

The bottom line is that you will never know what will best suit your child's teacher unless you have the respect and courtesy to send a timely email, ask the question politely, and don't expect them to be able to turn a meeting around in 24 hours.

Remember, if you are the one who is asking for an out-of-class-hours meeting, it's up to you to be flexible with its timing.

LETTING TEACHERS KNOW WHAT YOU WANT TO TALK ABOUT

It might be hard for you to believe, but just as some parents feel nervous about talking to teachers, some teachers worry about talking to parents. This usually isn't the case when conversations are planned in advance, but if parents have a habit of unexpectedly showing up and asking curly questions without notice, teachers' reluctance to engage with them is understandable.

Being randomly cornered in the carpark is undesirable, but what's even worse for off-duty teachers are the parental ambushes that happen when they are not at school and are spending private time with their loved ones. Ask any teacher you know if they've had a parent–teacher meeting in the cereal aisle at Coles with a mum or dad who just wouldn't take a hint – I'll bet they'll have more than one tale to tell you.

As the parent of a sensitive child with unique needs, you may need to talk with your child's teacher now and then next year, and if that's the case you will not want to be the parent that the teacher avoids. Making sure the teacher doesn't run in the other direction when they see you in the playground doesn't take much. All you need to remember is these three things:

- Before the meeting, let them know what you want to talk about.
- During the meeting, stick to the subject.
- After the meeting, thank the teacher for their time.

These days most teachers have a professional email address they use for work purposes. If you want to catch up with your child's teacher, simply drop them a line and politely ask for a meeting.

The best times to talk to teachers

You might like to use words like:

> *Hi Ms Jones,*
>
> *Selena has been telling me all about the things she's been learning in class lately. I really appreciate the support you've given to her. I wonder if you might have some time in the next couple of weeks to catch up with me. I'd like to share some results that have just arrived from Selena's speech pathologist and see if there is anything extra I can be doing at home to support the work you're doing at school to improve Selena's reading. The best days for me are Tuesday and Thursday, however I know that you're busy, and if you have any time at all I will make sure I'm available. Thanks so much, and I look forward to hearing from you at your convenience …*

When you send a message like this, your child's teacher will appreciate your courtesy and will usually get back to you as quickly as they can.

When the day of the meeting comes, the teacher will also appreciate it when you arrive prepared and ready to discuss the topic you outlined in your email. It's not fair to lure a teacher into a meeting that is supposedly about one subject only to launch into several issues they had no warning of; if you do this, be prepared for the fact that it might be the last meeting the teacher makes themselves available for with you for a while.

A quick note of thanks is always a nice way to acknowledge the time and effort the teacher took to meet with you. If you want to make sure the teacher will talk with you again, don't forget to send a quick follow-up message that expresses your gratitude.

FIRST AND LAST WEEK FAILS

As Sam mentioned, the very first week of school is not always a great time for teachers to have one-on-one meetings with parents, because children have not yet settled into routines, and the dynamics of the classroom are not yet established. Teachers can't talk about something they have yet to observe, and can share much deeper insights if they have a bit of time to work with your child before they speak with you about how things are going in the classroom and playground.

The last week of the term can be pretty fraught too. You might be surprised by how exhausted your little one will be at the end of the five-day-a-week routine, let alone ten consecutive weeks of Monday to Friday school days. By week nine or ten of the term, everyone – including teachers and parents – is just hanging on until the school holidays arrive. If you really want to have a sensible conversation with the teacher, try to avoid the last week of term, for their sake and yours.

AVOIDING REPORT TIME

Next year, you are likely to receive a written report from your child's school at the end of term two and at the end of term four. While report writing is part of a teacher's job, it's a task that can't be done during class time. Most teachers usually write reports when their students have left for the day or at home, so don't be surprised if finding a mutually convenient time to catch up for a private parent–teacher chat is tricky at these two points in the year.

Week seven of terms two and four is when principals usually require teachers to submit student reports for review. Parents who are primary school veterans often know that this is not the week in which to schedule after-school meetings with classroom teachers, and as

The best times to talk to teachers

you'll be a newcomer next year, hopefully this 'inside information' will help you.

If you can wait until after reports are written, you'll often find that the teacher who has just done a full analysis of your child's performance will be perfectly placed to talk with you. Your respect for the busy period before reports are issued will be appreciated by your child's teacher, so if you are in doubt about the best time to meet, simply send an email to the teacher and make a polite enquiry. The teacher will let you know what works for them.

CHAPTER 17

WHO'S WHO AT SCHOOL?

> 'At pick-up time, the mums would gather for a chat and there was one mum who always made her presence felt. Her son had additional needs, which was fine with everyone, but she would often tell us about all the things at school that she wasn't happy with. She seemed to spend lots of time making complaints in the principal's office, and I wouldn't have blamed the teachers if they gave her a wide berth. Eventually, that's what the other mums and I did.'
>
> *Mandy, Charli's mum*

Sometimes I really feel for school principals. Their position at the top of the tree in schools means some parents think of them as the obvious go-to person whenever they have a question or concern. At the start of the year, their phones run hot with queries, and a lot of their time is taken calming frayed nerves and answering questions that someone else on the school's staff may have been better equipped for.

As a parent who is new to the school, it's probably natural for you to gravitate towards the person to whom you have already spoken about your sensitive child. You will want to make sure that your son or daughter is catered for, and who better to ask than the boss, right?

Well, maybe, but not always.

While the principal will probably be very interested in helping you and your child settle in to life at school, every organisation has its structure. Knowing how to navigate the one at your child's new school will make a big difference to the way in which you and your child sail through next year.

THE PRINCIPAL'S ROLE

If the principal's friendly face, strong leadership style and apparent commitment to inclusion was a driving force in your decision to enrol your child at their new school then you are likely to feel quite an affinity for this dynamic educator. You may think of the principal as an ally in your effort to secure a safe and happy start for your child's schooling, and be looking forward to a long and productive partnership.

It might be a bit confusing, then, to get to school next year and find that the principal is not as available to you as you expected he or she was going to be. You might wonder why the principal is not in his or her office when you drop by to ask questions, or why reception staff direct you to the deputy principal or classroom teacher when you explain the reason for your visit.

Before you make a bee line to the principal's office next year in the way that Mandy's fellow mum did, remember that principals have complex and busy professional lives. They run the business end of the school, and while one minute they might be at the school gate welcoming children and parents at the start of the day, ten minutes later they could be dealing with complicated staffing, budget or building repair issues.

A principal's role involves a delicate balance of being there when people need them, but also delegating to other trusted and experienced teachers who have the knowledge and skill to run the day-to-day operations of the school. Don't be offended if, next year, the principal can't interrupt what he or she is doing to take your call. It's not personal, it's just that they only have so many hours in a day.

WHO ELSE CAN YOU CALL?

The great news is that, even if the principal is not available, there are usually lots of people in the school who will be more than happy to talk with you about your child next year. The best way to get answers to your questions or to convey your concerns is to make an appointment so that the time you have with the classroom teacher, learning support teacher, school counsellor or assistant principal is well spent.

Here's a quick summary of some of the key people you might want to talk to. Their roles are listed in ascending order, so start with the first one and move to the next level if you don't get what you need from your conversation.

Note that the principal isn't even on this list. Before you make an appointment to see the school's leader, do try to sort it out with someone else first. You never know when things will be so serious that you will have to go to the top of the tree. Hopefully this will rarely happen for your unique needs child, but for the best effect, you'll want to make taking issues to the principal the exception rather than the rule.

Role	You should call this person because …
Classroom teacher	Your child's classroom teacher should always be your first point of call when it comes to discussing your son's or daughter's experiences at school. Not only is it courteous to deal directly with the teacher who spends the majority of their day with your child, but if you handle it right, answers to your questions and advice about what you can be doing to support your child at home will be given directly to you, instead of by a third party. The classroom teacher is the one person who has an idea of how your child is going in the social, emotional and academic context of the classroom and playground. The best and most appropriate thing to do is send a quick email or make a phone call to request a meeting. Let the teacher know what you would like to talk about so that he or she can be prepared, and make sure you keep your intention to talk to the teacher private. In the early days of your relationship with the teacher and school, trust is being built on both sides. If you want the teacher to collaborate with you, try not to share the details of everything that is said and done with other parents. Gossip spreads quickly at the school gate and you might be surprised about how quickly word gets back to the teacher that you have been talking about them.

Who's who at school?

Role	You should call this person because...
Stage coordinator	If you feel awkward about talking with your child's classroom teacher, but don't want to be seen to be over-reacting, a stage coordinator may be able to help. The Australian curriculum is divided into 'stages', and next year your child will enter Stage One. Experienced teachers are often appointed to leadership roles, and you may find that your child's school has a stage coordinator who supports teaching and learning in Stage One. In some schools, stage coordinators look after several year groups, such as Kindergarten to Year Two, or Year Three to Year Six. A stage coordinator is likely to know your child and be a good person to chat to about your concerns. You can always approach staff who are higher up in the school hierarchy if you need to, but sometimes it's better for all concerned if you can resolve small issues without the added drama of getting your child's teacher's boss involved.
Learning Support Teacher	If you have questions about the provision of extra help in the classroom, the school's Learning Support Teacher can be a good person to ask. Learning Support Teachers often coordinate additional programs for children who are gifted, or for those who struggle because of language or early literacy difficulties. If you have concerns for your child's learning, it might be helpful to ask for a joint meeting with the classroom teacher and the Learning Support Teacher, so that you are all on the same page and that an understanding of strategies used at home and school can be developed.

Role	You should call this person because …
School counsellor	School counsellors are often trained psychologists who have a strong understanding of children's learning and behaviour. Their focus on supporting children's wellbeing means that helping children to manage the social and emotional demands of school is part of what they do. School counsellors often have years of experience dealing with families who are struggling with difficult circumstances, so it's quite likely they have assisted families like yours before. Depending on the situation, the school counsellor at your child's school could be involved with your child in a number of ways. He or she could conduct formal testing of your child's learning skills, or provide confidential counselling and problem-solving support to you and your child if life at home is a little rocky. It's worth keeping in mind that some schools 'share' their school counsellor with other neighbouring schools that are part of their network, so you might find your child's school only has the services of its school counsellor for a few days a week. If you think your child would benefit from the involvement of the school counsellor, call the school to find out when he or she will be there so that you can make an appointment for a confidential meeting.

Role	You should call this person because …
Assistant or deputy principal	Your child's new school is likely to have a deputy or assistant principal who is deeply involved in the daily operations of the school. Sometimes, these senior educators juggle classroom teaching roles with administrative responsibilities, so like everyone who works at a school, they are pretty busy. Deputy and assistant principals are sometimes the first people that children are sent to if there has been a problem in the classroom or playground. In some bigger schools, where there is more than one deputy or assistant principal, senior staff may also look after parent liaison duties for particular year groups too. These school leaders work closely with classroom teachers and are very likely to be aware of your child's unique needs, even if you and they have never spoken in the months before school began. Getting to know the deputy or assistant principal at your child's school is worth your while, because if something goes pear-shaped at school, he or she is likely to be the person who calls you. If the question or problem you have discussed with your child's classroom teacher has not been resolved, take it to the deputy or assistant principal before you make the call to the principal. Staff will appreciate the fact that you followed appropriate 'channels', and the outcome for you and your child will probably be better when you show your respect for the 'chain of command' in the school.

Role	You should call this person because …
Reception staff	As I mentioned earlier, the (usually) ladies who run the school office secretly run the school. Questions about logistics, lunchboxes and library bags can usually be answered by these experienced people who are often the heart and soul of the school. They deal with questions all day long, so one more from you is unlikely to be a problem for them, however it will ensure that, by asking the right questions of the right people, you build good relationships across the school which will benefit your child and family in the long run.

So, in summary, start with the classroom teacher and work your way up, using appropriate channels such as polite emails and phone calls. To get a quick resolution with minimal fuss, avoid involving the principal unless you really have to.

IT TAKES TWO TO HAVE A CONVERSATION

If you really want to be heard by the people who matter at your child's new school, understanding what is appropriate, who to talk to and how to have those conversations is important.

Hopefully, things will run smoothly for your sensitive child next year and you will rarely, if ever, have to escalate a problem through to the principal. That being said, if all of your efforts fail or if you have a very significant concern, the fact that you have followed protocols and conferred with staff in a respectful and collaborative manner will go a long way towards finding a resolution.

Remember, communication is a two-way thing. Being heard means that, as parents, we also need to be prepared to listen and to notice the cues we are given by teachers who, like us, only want the best for our children.

CHAPTER 18

TOP TIPS FOR PARENT–TEACHER INTERVIEWS

I've lost count of the number of parent–teacher meetings I've attended since I started teaching in 1988. Back then, I wasn't a parent, but I am one now, and because I've sat on both sides of the desk I know how stressful school meetings can be. For everyone.

As I have been writing this book, I've spoken to many teachers who are keen for parents to know one simple truth: they care for your child and want what is best for them.

Sometimes, this means having conversations with you that they would prefer not to have. It means telling you about problems you might prefer to avoid, and it occasionally means they need to listen to a perspective from you that they would prefer not to hear.

But for good teachers – caring and professional educators – hearing what you have to say and reflecting on how they, as a teacher, can make things better is part of the process.

The way you approach meetings with teachers is important too.

If you go in too 'gung-ho', there's a chance you'll alienate key staff whose support you really need. On the other hand, if you don't present your family's concerns effectively, problems have the potential to escalate and to negatively affect your child's learning and social and emotional wellbeing.

There's an art to having successful school meetings, and it can take years to perfect. I want to short cut that learning curve for you, so here are some of my top tips for having effective conversations with the staff at your child's new school.

Hopefully they'll help next year and in the years to come.

TOP TIP 1: SEND AN EMAIL FIRST

No teacher deserves to be ambushed at their classroom door by a parent hell bent on having a conversation the teacher didn't see coming. While 3.10 pm might be convenient for you to convene a spontaneous meeting, it could be the worst time possible for the teacher, who will no doubt want to talk with you in a respectful and professional way at a time that works for you both.

When it comes to meeting with your child's teacher, do the right thing.

If you have an issue, question or concern you would like to address, send an email or make a phone call to the school. Ask the teacher for a time to meet privately, and give them a brief idea of what you want to discuss.

Most teachers will be quite happy to catch up with you, but before they do, it will be helpful to know what you want to talk about so that they can investigate your query and be in a position to give you the most information possible about your child. Sometimes, the question you have might be easily dealt with by email and may not require a meeting. At other times, your concern might require the teacher to consult with colleagues or other parents.

Either way, it makes sense to not only have the courtesy to advise the teacher about the reason for your request, but to also allow some time for preparation to take place. This will mean you have the best chance possible of achieving an outcome that meets your child's unique needs.

TOP TIP 2: THE KISS PRINCIPLE

When communicating via email with teachers, keep it simple.

As much as they appreciate the time, effort and emotion that has gone into your carefully constructed 1000-word email epic, teachers are generally quite time-poor. They want to help, but time spent reading multi-page essays that ramble on and on could be better spent sourcing the support your sensitive child needs.

The best email to send to your child's teacher is a polite, succinct message that gets to the point and stays there.

Let the teacher know how they can contact you, and be prepared to wait a day or two for a reply. Remember, teachers' days are spent teaching children, not sitting at a computer answering correspondence. It may take them some time to get back to you, and this will especially be the case if your child's teacher works part time or holds a school leadership position.

TOP TIP 3: THE POWER OF A 'CC'

Emails are a fantastic way to communicate with teachers because they are quick and efficient, but it's easy for a teacher to miss a single email if they receive many messages every day. One way to

make sure your child's teacher never misses your message is to send a copy of it to another member of staff. This person, who is listed as a 'cc', will receive a 'carbon copy' of your message, and could be the teacher who job shares with the teacher you have written to, the assistant principal, Learning Support Teacher or another member of the school leadership team.

Regardless of who you 'cc', you will probably notice that you receive a timely response from your child's teacher because your message has been visible to one of their colleagues. This is a simple but effective way to ensure your message gets through and that school staff are accountable for their correspondence.

TOP TIP 4: NEVER MEET ALONE

Over the years, I've attended many a school meeting where I've been the lone parent in the room. It was always hard to keep my emotions in check when confronted by two, three or even more members of school staff who, in response to my advocacy for my son, prepared in advance for the meeting and took turns to execute the plan they had developed hours or even days before I arrived.

At times, I showed up for what I thought was a meeting with one teacher, only to discover that several members of the school executive had been invited without my knowledge. The sheer weight of numbers on the other side of the room meant that I invariably felt intimidated and uncertain. The outcome I hoped for rarely happened because teachers always had one another's backs, and even with my background, they invariably banded together in an effort to, metaphorically, roll over the top of me.

It was stressful and at times traumatic, and it took me years to realise that going to a meeting on my own put me at a natural disadvantage.

On the day I turned up at a school meeting with a support person of my own, the tide turned. In the years since, I have shared this tip with hundreds of parents, who have told me that it has made a huge difference to outcomes for their sensitive children and for their families.

This tip is a simple but important one. Never go to a meeting at school on your own.

Take a friend, colleague, neighbour or even your mum. It doesn't matter who accompanies you, but the sheer act of introducing your companion as 'my support person' puts teachers on notice that what is said and done in the meeting will have a witness.

It's important to emphasise that it's not appropriate for your support person to participate in the meeting, however by taking notes of what is said and by whom they fulfil an important function. Your support person's presence gives you the chance to fully engage in the conversation, and when you are speaking, your support person will be able to observe the reactions and interactions of school staff too. The record they take will help you to reflect on the outcome of the meeting and provide you with documentary evidence of what took place. Taking a support person with you may give you extra confidence, and the presence of your companion also sends a valuable message to the school that you consider the topic under discussion to be important.

Choose wisely

I have to tell you that I rarely took my Glasgow-born husband to school meetings. With a temper to match his red hair, the art of school-based diplomacy was lost on him, and he freely admits that he can be more of a hindrance than a help when conversations turn to contentious subjects. Having said that, there were times when having him there was important, because in articulating our child's

needs together we presented a united front that made it harder for school staff to label me as a 'helicopter' or 'lawnmower' parent. (In the privacy of the staffroom they may have done that anyway, but I usually got a better outcome from the meeting when I arrived with a 'plus one', and that was all that mattered.)

So the moral of the story is to take someone with you, if for no other reason than for moral support. As the parent of a sensitive child with unique needs, you deserve it.

TOP TIP 5: HELP ME TO UNDERSTAND

The phrase 'help me to understand' can change a conversation for the better, and I truly wish I had learned to use it earlier in my career.

Our sensitive children have their own vulnerabilities, and it's natural for parents like you and me to want to protect them from harm. We want other people to understand them as we do, and we want our concerns and needs to be heard and acknowledged.

In our quest for understanding, it's easy to head into a school meeting or start composing an email with one objective in mind: to make the teacher understand our point of view and to persuade them to do what we want them to do.

But when the conversation is about our unique child, the combination of emotions like fear, frustration and a sense of powerlessness can create a recipe for conflict and miscommunication. Words used carelessly, amid feelings of worry and uncertainty, make it easy for people on both sides of the conversation to be misunderstood.

That's why, if you take nothing else from this book, I hope that 'help me to understand' is one thing you will remember.

'Help me to understand' softens the tone of questions and gives the person who is speaking to you an opportunity to explain the circumstances surrounding a situation.

It allows you to set the tone for the conversation and shows the other party you are listening to them. It conveys the idea that you are open to having a respectful discussion, and it encourages them to take a similar approach.

'Help me to understand' stops process-driven teachers in their tracks, and in the heat of the moment, helps you to focus on the things that contributed to a situation rather than just the trigger for the problem.

Some examples

If you are called to a meeting at school to discuss your child's behaviour, you could open the conversation with, 'Help me to understand … What was happening just before this occurred?' or, 'Can you help me to understand? How did this all come about?'

If a teacher reports concerns about your child's learning or development, you could ask, 'Can you help me to understand what you have noticed and how it is affecting him?'

If a parent reports an altercation that has occurred in the playground with another child, you could ask, 'Okay. Help me to understand. What led up to this, and who else was involved?'

It works for teachers too

Teachers can use 'help me to understand' too.

In fact, if more teachers used this phrase at the start of their conversations with parents of children who have unique needs, the

relationships between them might be easier and communication more sensitive.

Who knows... maybe we can start something with these four words.

Please try using them.

You might be surprised by the way in which they change conversations, and relationships, for the better.

CONCLUSION

LIFEBOATS AND SAFETY NETS

Next year you and your child will begin a journey. It's a journey you can't really pack a bag for, because it's going to last for more than a decade and take you both to places you don't even know about yet.

Going to school is like going on a really slow round-the-world cruise. Some of the ports you will visit with your son or daughter will be full of exciting discoveries and moments of pure joy. But travel is a tricky thing, especially when you have kids in tow. There'll be times when you haven't got a clue what's going on. You can be guaranteed there'll be unexpected detours that weren't on the itinerary, and you and your child are likely to travel to places that you can't wait to leave as well.

Hundreds of other people will get on and off your child's school ship as the next few years go by. Captains, activities officers, deckhands and other passengers will all be part of the trip you are about to take, and each will play their part in getting your child to where they are going. You will get to know some of them well, and others will be faces in the crowd who will soon be forgotten. There may even be a few whose deck chairs you learn to actively avoid because their approach to the expedition is very different to yours.

Regardless of where your child's ship sails, at the end of the day your unique son or daughter will return to your cabin. They'll come home to you in your role as their own personal tour guide, porter, navigator and interpreter.

Next year, your sensitive child will begin a life-changing voyage, and along the way you'll not only be their safety net, but at times you might be their lifeboat too.

THE SHIP'S CAPTAIN

I often tell mums that we are the captain of the ship. We might be lucky enough to share the parenting journey with supportive partners, friends and relatives, but when the ship sets sail, we are the ones who stay on deck to make sure we don't hit an iceberg. If our reserves run low, there's a risk that everything will come to a grinding halt or that our family ship might sail seriously off course.

As the parent of a sensitive child who has unique needs, you're possibly already used to navigating your child's day, and you may even carry more than your fair share of the load yourself. Of course, most of the time your child is probably quite capable of walking alone and carrying a responsibility backpack of their own, but – as you and I know – there are moments when things go pear-shaped.

That's when we pick our kids up and carry them.

Next year, and in all of the years to come, there may be moments when your child needs you to do just that.

There will be times when you will need to make a judgement call about when to walk in front of them to show them the way and when to walk beside them to give them courage and confidence as they face a new challenge. There may even be times when you have to consciously decide to walk behind your child so you can catch them if they fall.

To be able to do these things, you'll need to make sure you're able to make sensible choices and are ready to bear the load at a moment's notice. Staying in good emotional shape yourself is going to be important, because the journey through school can be demanding.

As a parent, you'll be making decisions about your child's itinerary and maybe even dealing with people who don't understand your language. It's the language of a parent's love, but it's not always easily understood by others.

Taking moments for yourself and getting support when you need it is perfectly okay when you are on your voyage with your sensitive child. After all, sometimes the guidance of someone who's been there before is all you need to get back on course, so don't be afraid to ask for help now and in the future.

ELASTIC BAND KIDS

New interests, friends, skills and talents all lie ahead, waiting to be discovered, as your child departs on their journey to school. If you've ever been on a cruise ship, you'll know that they are filled with long corridors, hidden alcoves and decks with a view. Sometimes, parents travelling with their children know exactly where they are, and at other times they're not quite sure but hope and trust that they are safe.

Starting school is a little bit like that. Just as you take your child to Kids Club at the start of the cruising day and rely on the staff to make sure they don't fall overboard, so will you depend on teachers to look after your child's best interests when you're not there. Your trust muscles are going to get a workout in the next twelve months,

and there might even be moments of uncertainty when new people come into your child's life and start to influence your son or daughter in ways you didn't expect.

But remember, kids are like elastic bands.

They like to stretch and to see how far they can go on their own. Next year, you might start to feel this as your child starts to develop a sense of self that is separate from you. As your son or daughter gets older, there will be times when they pull away from you, but the key will be making sure that, when they need you, they can snap back in to the comfort and certainty of home.

Over the next decade or so, standing strong as a family will be the key to supporting your sensitive, unique child as they take the journey that is school. There will be times when you will be their safety net, catching them when they fall and showing them how to bounce back. There will times when you are their lifeboat, rowing out to save them when the waters get too rough or too deep and they are struggling to keep afloat.

When storms come and the seas of school are rough, the foundations of unconditional love that binds your family together will see you through until the tide turns.

Teachers, schools and classmates come and go, but family is for life.

Nurture yours, and do all that you can to let your son or daughter know that, no matter what, you've always got their back.

May the months ahead be full of memorable moments, and may you look back on this time of getting 'ready' for school with fondness and a touch of pride… not only in your son or daughter's achievements but also in your own.

You've got this, and I wish you and your sensitive child every success for the years ahead.

LOCAL EDUCATION AUTHORITIES

All Australian schools must meet the standards set by their relevant state or territory-based education authority. Many are part of education networks that regulate and resource the delivery of teaching and learning.

As the parent of a sensitive child who has unique needs, you may occasionally have cause to contact the agencies that set rules, make decisions or provide services that are related to your child's schooling.

In the following pages you will find a list of contact details for some of the major agencies in each state and territory in Australia for your use now and for future reference.

The details listed were current at the time of writing and include contacts for the head offices of:

- *State schools* – also known as 'government' or 'public' schools.

- *Catholic systemic schools* – faith-based schools that are part of a Catholic schools network.

- *Independent Schools associations* – organisations that represent member schools that are independent in structure and serve a range of communities of different types, sizes, religious affiliations and educational philosophies.

Australian Capital Territory

Type of school	Lead agency	Contact details
State (public) schools	*ACT Education Directorate*	*Head office location:* 220 Northbourne Avenue Braddon, ACT 2612 *Postal address:* GPO Box 158 Canberra, ACT 2601 *General phone enquiries:* (02) 6207 5111 *Website:* www.education.act.gov.au
Catholic (systemic) schools	*Catholic Education Office* (Archdiocese of Canberra and Goulbourn)	*Head office location:* 52–54 Franklin Street, Manuka, ACT 2603 *Postal address:* PO Box 3317 Manuka, ACT 2603 *General phone enquiries:* (02) 6234 5455 *General email address:* reception@cg.catholic.edu.au *Website:* www.cg.catholic.edu.au
Independent schools	*The Association of Independent Schools of the ACT*	*Head office location:* Unit 2, 16 Thesiger Court Deakin, ACT 2600 *Postal address:* PO Box 225 Deakin West, ACT 2600 *General phone enquiries:* (02) 6162 0834 *General email address:* aisact@ais.act.edu.au *Website:* www.ais.act.edu.au

Local education authorities

New South Wales

Type of school	Lead agency	Contact details
State (public) schools	*NSW Department of Education*	*Head office location:* 35 Bridge Street Sydney, NSW 2001 *Postal address:* GPO Box 33 Sydney, NSW 2001 *General phone enquiries:* 1300 679 332 *General email address:* DECinfo@det.nsw.edu.au *Website:* www.education.nsw.gov.au
Catholic (systemic) schools	*Catholic Schools NSW* There are 11 Diocesan Catholic Schools Authorities in NSW (commonly referred to as Catholic Education Offices), which provide direct administrative and educational support to the schools in their Diocese. Please contact your local CEO for details of your local Catholic schools.	*Head office location:* Level 9, Polding Centre 133 Liverpool Street Sydney, NSW 2001 *Postal address:* PO Box 20768 World Square, NSW 2002 *General phone enquiries:* (02) 9287 1555 *Website:* www.csnsw.catholic.edu.au
Independent schools	*The Association of Independent Schools of NSW*	*Head office location:* Level 12, 99 York Street Sydney, NSW 2000 *Postal address:* Level 12, 99 York Street Sydney, NSW 2000 *General phone enquiries:* (02) 9299 2845 *Website:* www.aisnsw.edu.au

Northern Territory

Type of school	Lead agency	Contact details
State (public) schools	Northern Territory Department of Education	*Head office location:* Mitchell Centre, 55–59 Mitchell Street Darwin, NT 0800 *Postal address:* GPO Box 4821 Darwin, NT 0801 *General phone enquiries:* (08) 8999 5659 *General email address:* infocentre.det@nt.gov.au *Website:* www.education.nt.gov.au
Catholic (systemic) schools	Catholic Education Northern Territory (Diocese of Darwin)	*Head office location:* 17 Beaton Road Berrimah, NT 0828 *Postal address:* PO Box 219 Berrimah, NT 0828 *General phone enquiries:* (08) 8984 1400 *General email address:* admin.ceo@nt.catholic.edu.au *Website:* www.ceont.catholic.edu.au
Independent schools	Association of Independent Schools of the Northern Territory	*Head office location:* Level 2, NAB Building 71 Smith Street Darwin, NT 0801 *Postal address:* GPO Box 2085 Darwin, NT 0801 *General phone enquiries:* (08) 8981 8668 *General email address:* accounts@aisnt.asn.au *Website:* www.aisnt.asn.au

Queensland

Type of school	Lead agency	Contact details
State (public) schools	Queensland Department of Education and Training	Head office location: 30 Mary Street Brisbane, Qld 4000 Postal address: PO Box 15033 City East, Qld 4002 General phone enquiries: 13 74 68 General email address: Enquiries.SchoolOperations@det.qld.gov.au Website: www.education.qld.gov.au
Catholic (systemic) schools	Queensland Catholic Education Commission There are 22 Diocesan Catholic Schools Authorities in QLD (commonly referred to as Catholic Education Authorities), which provide direct administrative and educational support to the schools in their Diocese. Please contact your local CEA for details of your local Catholic schools.	Head office location: Penola Place Level 1/143 Edward Street Brisbane, Qld 4000 Postal address: GPO Box 2441 Brisbane, Qld 4001 General phone enquiries: (07) 3316 5800 General email address: enquiries@qcec.catholic.edu.au Website: www.qcec.catholic.edu.au
Independent schools	Independent Schools Queensland	Head office location: First Floor, 96 Warren Street Spring Hill, Qld 4000 Postal address: PO Box 957 Spring Hill, Qld 4004 General phone enquiries: (07) 3228 1515 General email address: office@isq.qld.edu.au Website: www.isq.qld.edu.au

South Australia

Type of school	Lead agency	Contact details
State (public) schools	South Australia Department for Education	Head office location: 31 Flinders Street Adelaide, SA 5000 Postal address: GPO Box 1152 Adelaide, SA 5001 General phone enquiries: (08) 8226 1000 General email address: decdcustomers@sa.gov.au Website: www.education.sa.gov.au
Catholic (systemic) schools	Catholic Education South Australia (CESA) 103 Catholic schools are supported by CESA. Please check the website for a school that is located near you.	Head office location: 116 George Street Thebarton, SA 5031 Postal address: PO Box 179 Torrensville Plaza, SA 5031 General phone enquiries: (08) 8301 6600 General email address: director@cesa.catholic.edu.au Website: www.cesa.catholic.edu.au
Independent schools	Association of Independent Schools of South Australia	Head office location: 301 Unley Road Malvern, SA 5061 Postal address: 301 Unley Road Malvern, SA 5061 General phone enquiries: (08) 8179 1400 General email address: office@ais.sa.edu.au Website: www.ais.sa.edu.au

Tasmania

Type of school	Lead agency	Contact details
State (public) schools	*Department of Education – Tasmania*	*Head office location:* 4 Salamanca Place Hobart, Tas. 7000
		Postal address: GPO Box 169 Hobart, Tas. 7001
		General phone enquiries: 1800 816 057
		General email address: ServiceCentre@education.tas.gov.au
		Website: www.education.tas.gov.au
Catholic (systemic) schools	*Catholic Education Office*	*Head office location:* 5 Emmett Place New Town, Tas. 7008
		Postal address: PO Box 102 North Hobart, Tas. 7002
		General phone enquiries: (03) 6210 8888
		Website: www.catholic.tas.edu.au
Independent schools	*Independent Schools Tasmania*	*Head office location:* Level 3/33 Salamanca Place Hobart, Tas. 7000
		Postal address: PO Box 616 Sandy Bay, Tas. 7005
		General phone enquiries: (03) 6224 0125
		General email address: admin@independentschools.tas.edu.au
		Website: www.independentschools.tas.edu.au

Victoria

Type of school	Lead agency	Contact details
State (public) schools	*Department of Education and Training Victoria*	Head office location: 2 Treasury Place East Melbourne, Vic. 3002 Postal address: GPO Box 4367 Melbourne, Vic. 3001 General phone enquiries: (03) 9637 2000 General email address: servicedesk@edumail.vic.gov.au Website: www.education.vic.gov.au/school
Catholic (systemic) schools	*Catholic Education Commission of Victoria* There are four Diocesan Catholic Education Offices in Victoria which provide direct administrative and educational support to the schools in their Diocese. Please contact your local CEO for details of your local Catholic schools.	Head office location: James Goold House 228 Victoria Parade East Melbourne, Vic. 3002 Postal address: PO Box 3 East Melbourne, Vic. 3002 General phone enquiries: (03) 9267 0228 General email address: secretary@cecv.catholic.edu.au Website: www.cecv.catholic.edu.au
Independent schools	*Independent Schools Victoria*	Head office location: 40 Rosslyn Street West Melbourne, Vic. 3003 Postal address: PO Box 119 North Melbourne, Vic. 3051 General phone enquiries: (03) 9825 7200 General email address: enquiries@is.vic.edu.au Website: www.is.vic.edu.au

Local education authorities

Western Australia

Type of school	Lead agency	Contact details
State (public) schools	*Western Australian Department of Education*	*Head office location:* 151 Royal Street East Perth, WA 6004 *General phone enquiries:* (08) 9264 4111 *Website:* www.education.wa.edu.au
Catholic (systemic) schools	*Catholic Education Western Australia* There are four Diocesan Catholic Education Offices in Western Australia which provide direct administrative and educational support to the schools in their Diocese. Please contact your local CEO for details of your local Catholic schools.	*Head office location:* 50 Ruislip Street Leederville, WA 6007 *Postal address:* PO Box 198 Leederville, WA 6903 *General phone enquiries:* (08) 6380 5200 *Website:* www.ceo.wa.edu.au
Independent schools	*Association of Independent Schools of Western Australia*	*Head office location:* Suite 3/41 Walters Drive Osborne Park, WA 6017 *Postal address:* PO Box 1817 Osborne Park DC, WA 6916 *General phone enquiries:* (08) 9441 1600 *General email address:* reception@ais.wa.edu.au *Website:* www.ais.wa.edu.au

HELPFUL RESOURCES

If you'd like to dive a bit deeper into some of the ideas, information and strategies mentioned in this book, the resources below are a good place to start.

Anxiety
Helping Your Anxious Child: A step-by-step guide for parents
Ronald Rapee, Susan Spence, Vanessa Cobham, Ann Wignall
New Harbinger Publications (2000)

The Highly Sensitive Child
Dr Elaine Aron
HarperCollins Publishers (2012)

What's Worrying You?
Molly Potter
Bloomsbury Publishing (2018)

Feeding
Raising a Healthy, Happy Eater: A parent's handbook
Nimali Fernado and Melanie Potock
The Experiment (2015)

The Great Food Explorer (music CD)
Dr Kay Toomey and Coles Whalen
http://sosapproach-conferences.com/product/music-cd/

Sensory processing
The Whole-Brain Child: 12 revolutionary strategies to nurture your child's developing mind
Daniel Siegel and Tina Bryson
Delacorte Press (2011)

The Out of Sync Child: Recognizing and coping with sensory processing disorder
Carol Stock Kranowitz
Skylight Press (2005)

Sensational Kids: Hope and help for children with sensory processing disorder (SPD)
Lucy Jane Miller
Pedigree Books (2014)

Raising a Sensory Smart Child: The definitive handbook for helping your child with sensory processing issues
Lindsey Biel
Penguin Putnam (2009)

Toileting
The Continence Foundation of Australia
www.continence.org.au/pages/children.html

Tips for Toilet Training: A guide for parents and professionals toilet training children with an autism spectrum disorder
www.suelarkey.com.au/product/tips-for-toileting/

A FEW WORDS OF THANKS

When I was a classroom teacher, a childhood photo taken by my mother used to sit on my desk in the staffroom. The snapshot showed me playing 'schools', and is possibly one of the most revealing photos that's ever been taken of me.

A confident two year old, I was clearly in my element. With my blackboard, teddies and little brother, Ian, seated just out of shot, I pretended to be a teacher while he dutifully obeyed my every command. Eventually, Ian discovered that Matchbox cars were much more fun than his bossy big sister, but for a while there, I was living the dream.

Being a teacher was all I ever really wanted to be, and more than 40 years on, I can honestly say that I wouldn't have had it any other way.

But the opportunities I've had to reach my goals have not been the result of anything special on my part. They've come about because of the support, understanding and inspiration that has been gifted to me over many years by amazing people who have walked by my side.

Without them, my path could have been very different, and this book would have told a very different story.

Many of you will know who you are, but just in case you don't, allow me to say a word of thanks.

> To you, my Kids First Children's Services colleagues both present and past, for your vision, skill and hard work. It is an honour to share what I do with you.
>
> To you, Aisling Graham, James Bawtree, Andrew Griffiths, Glen Carlson and Michael Hanrahan for being key people of influence and encouraging me to take a leap of faith.
>
> To you, Tracey Nicholls, Lisa Neate, Michele Reynolds, Susan Sorenson, Kathrin Schicke, Karen Bucknell and Susie MacPherson, for generously sharing your educational expertise as this book has taken shape.
>
> To you, Dr Kay Toomey, Dr Amanda Mergler and Roger Torbert, for permitting me to share your professional wisdom.
>
> To you, Christine Gardner, Sarah Ambrose and Denise Wright, for your dedication, sensitivity and commitment to your profession. Any child lucky enough to be in your classroom is fortunate indeed.
>
> To you, Marama Carmichael, for sharing my journey, being there to fix what I break and bringing the big picture to life online.
>
> To you, Kylie Ouvrier and all of the other Kids First mums who have allowed me to share their children's stories. You inspire me with your tenacity, optimism and love for your kids.
>
> To you, Pam MacLeod, for giving my family and me hope for the future when we needed it most.

To you, my Inner Circle, for the ride from the school gate to graduation and life in the big wide world. May we always see the funny side and never lose our love for a cheese platter.

To you, Debbie and Kim, for being my 'sistas from another mista' and for never failing to have my back, tell me straight and catch me before I fall.

To you, Leeta Caiger, for the precious gift of lifelong friendship and knowing me better than I know myself.

To you, Leah Milton, for raising me up and reminding me that what will be, will be.

To you, Bill and Carole Barry, for being the world's most wonderful parents and role models, and for instilling in me the core values of care, kindness, compassion and making a contribution that are so much of who I am.

To you, George Walker, for your rock solid belief, support and faith in me. This flight was not the one you boarded more than 20 years ago, but even in the most turbulent of times, you've held my hand and never let go. I love you.

And to you, Cameron Walker, for being the boy who inspired it all. I am, and always will be, proud of you. It is a privilege to be your mum.

ABOUT SONJA WALKER

Sonja Walker is the founder of Kids First Children's Services, an award-winning paediatric health and education practice in Sydney that has supported more than 11,000 children and families in the last 11 years.

At Kids First, Sonja leads an experienced team of psychologists, speech pathologists, occupational therapists and teachers. Together, they support children aged 2 to 18 as they get ready to meet the social, emotional and learning demands of preschool, school and life.

A qualified teacher for 30 years, Sonja is a strong and respected advocate for children and families. She is particularly committed to supporting children with additional needs, and served for several years on the board of children's charity Lifestart. She is also well known for her leadership of Kids First's popular free Community Service Seminar program, which has provided thousands of parents with opportunities to meet and learn from experts in the field of children's learning, behaviour and development.

At the heart of everything Sonja does is her role as the proud mum of a child with unique needs who has successfully navigated transitions to and from primary and high school. Sonja has sat on both sides of the desk at parent–teacher interviews and knows exactly what it feels like to be desperately worried about a son or daughter who is falling behind. Because of the unique insight she has into the perspectives of both parents and teachers, she is deeply committed to equipping parents with the knowledge and resources they need to support their kids.

Her commonsense approach, backed up by years of experience and the clinical expertise of the Kids First team, make her a sought-after writer, speaker and media commentator. Sonja also presents engaging, practical workshops and conference keynote presentations for a variety of audiences in corporate, early childhood and school settings across Australia.

As a working mum, Sonja understands the pressures of modern family life. She believes that every child deserves to be seen as an individual with unique and valuable gifts. She also believes in the right of every parent to be an involved and informed champion for their child. Her mission is to help kids of all ages and abilities to thrive and not just cope, and her passion is empowering parents to become strong and confident advocates for their kids.

For more information please visit www.kids-first.com.au or www.sonjawalker.com.au

COMING SOON

COMING SOON

www.ingramcontent.com/pod-product-compliance
Lightning Source LLC
Chambersburg PA
CBHW071231080526
44587CB00013BA/1568